THE UGLY PALACES

Safe upon the solid rock the ugly houses stand:
Come and see my shining palace built upon the sand!

Edna St. Vincent Millay

ROBERT A. LISTON

THE UGLY PALACES
HOUSING IN AMERICA

FRANKLIN WATTS, INC. | NEW YORK | 1974

Copyright © 1974 by Robert A. Liston
Printed in the United States of America
Design by Rafael Hernandez

Library of Congress Cataloging in Publication Data
Liston, Robert A
   The ugly palaces.
   SUMMARY: Surveys housing in the U.S.A.: its
problems, solutions that have been tried and failed, and
proposals offering us hope for the future.
   Bibliography: p.
   1. Housing—United States—Juvenile literature.
2. Public housing—United States—Juvenile literature.
[1. Housing]   I. Title.
HD7290.L57   301.5′4′0973   74-1044
ISBN 0-531-02673-6

To William E. Stone

CONTENTS

The difficulty in writing about the housing problem is that it won't sit quietly, in a vacuum, to be scrutinized. Other problems keep jostling it about. To write about housing, an author must inevitably write about poverty and urban problems, with a good deal of sociology and a smattering of history, politics, and economics thrown in.

A second difficulty is the extreme topicalness of the subject. Perhaps more than any other book I have written, I found myself constantly amending what I had written because of a headline in the newspaper. For example, most of the book was written when President Richard M. Nixon announced his freeze on federal housing spending and proposed broad cuts in housing funds in his 1974 budget. Then came the Watergate scandals with their massive erosion of Mr. Nixon's prestige and the effectiveness of his presidency at the outset of his second term, and the onset of the "energy crisis" with its unknown but possibly significant effect on the entire economy, including the housing industry. This book includes all of these matters.

I am indebted to many people, but most especially Eleanor R. Seagraves of Washington, D.C., Richard Gilman of Trumbull, Connecticut, William Boucher III of Baltimore, and David O. Strickland of Pensacola, Florida, who provided me with a great deal of material. I would also like to extend a general but nonetheless sincere thank you to the many bankers, real estate people, other experts, and ordinary homeowners and renters who supplied information and opinions.

Trumbull, Connecticut

INTRODUCTION

THE PROBLEM

PART ONE

A STRANGE PROBLEM

CHAPTER ONE

A Strange Problem

The United States has few problems more complex or less amenable to solution than proper housing for all its citizens. As the world's wealthiest nation, we have tried for almost forty years to meet a legislated goal of providing a decent home for everyone; we have spent hundreds of billions of dollars toward that end. And our principal accomplishment has been to make the problem worse.

The nature and depth of the housing problem can be illustrated by some items based upon news reports.

* Workmen began in 1972 to dynamite and demolish some of the thirty-three high-rise apartment buildings of the Pruitt-Igoe public housing project in St. Louis. Built in the 1950's, its design had won an architectural award and it was hailed as a "new pattern" for solving the problem of slum housing. Twenty years later it had become a sorry scene of crime, drug addiction, and vandalism. By January, 1972, over three-quarters of the buildings were abandoned, sealed with steel plates, and fenced to thwart vandals. Only 600 of the project's 2,870 apartments were occupied—and those residents were eager to move out. Federal officials reluctantly admitted the best use of Pruitt-Igoe, now, was as an experiment in ways to demolish structurally sound buildings. Several million dollars were being spent for tearing down what had been so hopefully built.

* Late in 1972, George Romney, secretary of Housing and Urban Development (HUD) in the cabinet of President Richard M. Nixon, announced his retirement. For four years he had struggled with the housing problem. He had been considered dedicated, even inspirational in the field, and during his time in office many innovative programs were begun. Yet, he quit in failure and publicly recommended that all federal housing programs be scrapped and that the nation begin all over again with new approaches. "We can no longer afford $100 billion mistakes," he said. This is the amount government officials estimate current federal housing programs will cost.

* A family consisting of a husband, wife, and their five children live in a fourth floor apartment of an old brownstone house in Harlem, New York City. The paint is peeling, the water is more often cold than warm, the toilet has a tendency to overflow, and the heat is uncertain at best. They have triple locks on the door to keep the addicts who sleep in the hallway from breaking in. The husband is employed, earning $95 a week in a dry cleaning establishment, but the family can afford no better place to live. They have applied for admission to a public housing project, but there is a long waiting list for the few apartments large enough to house a family of this size.

* A family in Detroit took advantage of a federal housing subsidy and purchased an older home which had been inspected by government experts and declared repaired and ready for occupancy. When cold weather came, the family discovered the roof leaked and the furnace needed to be replaced. Unable to afford the repairs, the family simply abandoned the house and their small investment in it. The federal government was stuck with a house no one wanted, on which the taxpayers had guaranteed a $20,000 mortgage plus interest.

* Plans were announced to build a public housing project in the white middle class Forest Hills section of New York City. Residents became greatly alarmed. They met, organized, staged demonstrations, and took court action to block the project. There was some violence.

* In November, 1972, *The New York Times* reported that nearly all of the nation's 3,000 local housing authorities were losing money. If more federal funds were not forthcoming, some of them would go bankrupt. It was reported by the *Times* that "many local authorities foresee a continuing circle of reduced maintenance and repairs, increased vacancies, further decline in income, and the creation of new slums where millions have been spent to remove old ones."

* There are 4.7 million housing units in the United States which lack complete plumbing (6 percent of all U.S. housing units). More than half of those sanitation time bombs are in the Southern states, mostly in rural areas.

* In 1970, the United States had 68.7 million housing units. Every twelfth one of those homes or apartments was considered substandard by the federal government because of overcrowding, that is, more than one person occupied each room.

Such a listing of facts and illustrations could go on and on but neither singly nor in series could they truly describe the housing problem. It is like studying an ocean by visiting an aquarium. The parts, while true, do not describe the whole.

We will make the first step toward solving the housing problem in America if we go to some pains to describe what the problem is. Indeed, as Secretary Romney suggested, we have thrown immense sums of money into housing without ever really understanding the basic problem. Thus what we did about it, though well-intentioned, never got to the root of the matter.

Shelter probably ranks third behind food and clothing among the basic needs of mankind, and there are those who would argue that shelter is more important than clothing. But simple shelter from the cold and rain and a place to sleep is hardly what man has in mind when he speaks of housing. Even cavemen elaborately decorated the walls and ceiling of their rocky abodes—simple shelter is not a home.

There is really no shortage of actual "places to live" in the United States. Except for a minor number of skid row derelicts, few if any Americans are forced to live out-of-doors for want of shelter, as hundreds of thousands do in India and other impoverished, greatly overcrowded nations.

According to a report by Donald D. Steward and Paul R. Myers of the federal Economic Research Service, the United States actually has a great deal of housing that is not lived in. Of the 68.7

million housing units in 1970, over 5.2 million (or 7.6 percent) were unoccupied. About two million of these were for sale or rent. Another million were used as seasonal or migratory housing. The remaining 2.1 million were described as "not actively on the market for occupancy." Steward and Myers suggested that some repairs and renovation would doubtless be needed on this vast supply of vacant housing, but all, or nearly all, could be made into acceptable quarters.

Even more startling, the United States builds new housing on a truly massive scale. In 1971 and again in 1972 well over two million new housing units were begun. Added to that, approximately a half million mobile homes were built in each of those years. The housing problem in the United States is most definitely not an overall housing shortage.

Indeed, impressive statistics can be cited which would seem to indicate that the United States has no such thing as a housing problem. During much of his time at HUD, Secretary Romney was fond of citing the success of the nation's housing efforts, calling it a "remarkable success story" on an "overall basis." In a speech to the National Association of Building Manufacturers in April, 1972 (only a few months before he quit) he ticked off these facts:

The 1970 census showed America had 69,000,000 housing units. That was a 50 percent increase over the number of units we had in 1950, while population growth during the same twenty-year period was about one-third. At today's record pace of homebuilding, we are now producing about two units for every new household. . . .

Almost two-thirds of our families are homeowners, and single-family houses still account for over two-thirds of our housing inventory. More housing was produced in 1971 than ever before in our history. I expect 1972 to add a new record.

More housing for low and moderate income families has been

> *funded and started in the past three years than in the previous thirty-one years.*
>
> *That list of statistics does not represent a picture of a housing crisis. Rather it represents a picture of success in providing decent housing for our people. The American people, generally speaking, are better housed than any people, present or past (author's emphasis).*

The common experience of most Americans would lead them to agree with Mr. Romney's evaluation. The majority of Americans live in tidy suburbs or neat little towns filled with row upon row of spotless homes on which great pride, affection, and expense have been lavished. For such Americans the biggest housing problem is killing the crabgrass and making the mortgage payment.

The dream of perhaps every American is a home of his own; and after the first home, a bigger and better one—it is part of the American ethic that a man's success and, indeed, his character are most visibly measured by the size and appurtenances of his dwelling place. A great many of us *have* succeeded in making our dreams come true.

We arrive, thus, at an anomaly in which Mr. Romney states on the one hand that we are generally the best housed nation in the history of the world, and on the other that he is resigning in discouragement over the failure of the nation's housing programs. This sounds foolish, but Mr. Romney, a most concerned, dedicated, and able citizen, is neither a fool nor a charlatan. He is aware that the word *housing* as in "housing problem" is a misnomer. It is a euphemism for some devilishly difficult social problems centered around poverty, race, education, employment, transportation, and crime.

The problem is not houses, as such. There are brownstones in New York, marble-stepped rowhouses in Baltimore, clapboard houses in St. Louis that are considered the apex of luxury and elegant living, while a few blocks away markedly similar houses are considered slums. Drive through New England and you will see old houses abandoned, falling down, eyesores. But you will also see whole villages of stately, century-old homes that are a picture postcard come to life.

A house or apartment, after all, is an inanimate object. It is an arrangement of wood and metal and plaster and glass and similar lifeless materials into a certain design. It takes on life and character only by the people who live in it. It is *people* who make homes, not houses. Our so-called housing problem is really a people problem.

There are those—legions of them—who will disagree with that statement. Indeed, our basic national approach to the difficult social problems of America has been the belief that houses change and improve people. The assumption is that if a person or family lives in modern, functional house or apartment, he will enjoy greater health and safety and be imbued with greater pride, industriousness, and well-being.

There is undoubtedly some element of truth in that idea. If a person loves his home, thinks it beautiful and enjoys living in it, he is surely happier. But for the federal government to build a $100 billion housing program on that precept, while ignoring such factors as employment, education, and neighborhoods, leads to the sort of discouraging results Mr. Romney found.

Viewing structures as inanimate objects, there is bad housing in the United States which ought to be destroyed. The federal government uses two criteria for determining substandard living space. Such housing either lacks complete plumbing or it is occupied by more than one person per room. The Steward and Myers study offers surprising information on where these substandard dwellings are and thereby helps to define the housing problem.

In 1970, there were 4.7 million housing units without complete plumbing, that is, hot and cold piped water inside the house, a

flush toilet, and a bath or shower for exclusive use of the occupants.

Of these 4.7 million units with inadequate plumbing, 3.8 million were occupied.

The South contained 55 percent of all the units; the North Central region, 23 percent; the Northeast, 14 percent; and the West, 8
percent.

The plumbingless houses are predominantly rural, with two out
of three located outside of metropolitan areas. Of all rural housing,
12 percent lacked full plumbing, while only 3.2 percent of urban
housing was so deficient.

Even though most of this unsanitary housing was occupied by
whites, such housing is more usually suffered by black people. Of
the 6.3 million black-occupied units in the nation, 17 percent
lacked plumbing. Of the 57 million white-occupied units, only
4.7 percent lacked full plumbing.

Of the 5.2 million overcrowded housing units in America, most,
by number, were located in cities, simply because 70 percent of all
Americans are urban dwellers. Yet, percentage-wise, overcrowding is more prevalent in rural areas, with 9.1 percent of all rural
houses being overcrowded, compared to 7.8 percent of all urban
housing units.

We tend to think of the housing problem in the United States as
an urban problem, using such words as slum and ghetto. But most
of the really bad, unsanitary housing in the United States which
ought to be destroyed and replaced is located in rural areas. The
statement has been made many times that a good deal of the much
discussed ghetto housing is no longer substandard. Most of the
truly unlivable urban housing has been abandoned or torn down
for housing developments, highways, and other public projects.

For the most part, the buildings in the slums are structurally
sound, with full plumbing, adequate wiring, and a tight roof. And
some, like Pruitt-Igoe in St. Louis, are relatively new and winners

of architectural prizes. The rural sharecropper with a dirt floor and an outdoor privy might long for as much. Yet, new housing or not, the urban ghettos and slums are there all right, festering social sores of unemployment, crime, addiction, disease, folly, disappointment, and despair.

The evidence is overwhelming: the "housing" problem doesn't have very much to do with houses per se. It does have a lot to do with money, which we take up next.

WHY HOUSING IS EXPENSIVE

CHAPTER TWO

In April, 1972, a man named Harold B. Finger journeyed to St. Louis. He was assistant secretary for research and technology of the Department of Housing and Urban Development, and he delivered the keynote address to the Second International Conference on Lower-Cost Housing of the American Society for Public Administration. Early in his remarks, Mr. Finger said:

"I must confess that I thought it a bit ironic that your keynote speaker should be from a nation which really does not have low cost housing."

A person may not have to be King Midas to buy a new house in America, but it helps if he owns stock in a gold mine. The median cost nationwide of a new house in February, 1972, was $26,200—a price that went up $2,000 in just one year.

In his speech, Mr. Finger listed some other statistics which illuminate just how high low-cost housing is in America.

* In 1960, two-thirds of all single family houses sold in the United States cost under $20,000. By 1970, sales of $20,000 houses had shrunk to 28 percent of the market.

* In 1970, the cost of a quarter acre of land, on the average, was $6,100—up 77 percent in a half decade.

* In 1970, the cost, including land, of the average single family home insured by the Federal Housing Administration was $25,000—an increase of 67 percent in five years.

* The total monthly housing expense for such an FHA house in 1970 had risen 85 percent in five years to $272.

* On the average, the local property taxes payable on the house and land had risen 85 percent in the five years.

These alarmingly high figures mentioned by Mr. Finger had increased even more by 1973. The high cost of housing in the United States has important ramifications for the entire fabric of American life. Before considering these, however, we need to ask why housing costs are so high.

This is a thicket prickly with the thorns of controversy. The rising costs involve business, labor, banks and building and loan associations, politics, government policy, lawyers, and the real estate industry.

Controversy results because everyone recognizes that housing costs are high and that there is a high level of public antagonism toward the rising prices. All of those involved in driving prices ever higher have a tendency to explain their actions by blaming someone else. We can try to wend our way through the thicket unscratched by avoiding blame and concentrating on some rather simple facts.

Basic American attitudes have led to high housing costs. The desire (perhaps *need* is not too strong a word) of Americans for land and a home of their own is deep in the national character. Land hunger motivated the first colonists; it drove generations of Americans, including millions of immigrants, to conquer and settle the successive frontiers. The frontier is long gone in America (with the exception of Alaska) but the same land hunger has driven tens of millions of Americans into the suburban greenswards to put their money down on a spot of land they can call their own.

The settlers on the frontier endured some incredible hardships to satisfy their hunger for land—perilous journeys by covered wagon, backbreaking work against hostile elements, and, usually, poverty. An analogy to today's suburbanites cannot be too closely drawn but the residents of the suburbs do endure perilous journeys by car to and from their places of employment, long traffic jams, and, as will be suggested, a form of poverty.

This need for a "place of their own" at almost any price has also been the foundation for the basic premise on which the whole housing industry has operated since 1945: *real estate prices will continue to rise.* This belief affects every facet of the industry. Suppliers of everything—from wooden planks to polished furniture, bricks to exotic floor tiles, copper pipe to indoor-outdoor thermometers—work on the premise that the home owner will pay for it. Labor unions bargain for higher wages, insurance companies raise their rates, lawyers charge more for title searches, and legislators vote increases in property taxes, all in the belief that, because of his desire for land, the home owner will pay and pay. Banks and other lending institutions make high risk loans which they would not even have considered a generation ago—asking for little or no down payment—either because the loan is insured by the federal government or because of their conviction that rising real estate prices will wipe out any risk of loss. If the home owner defaults on his payments and the lending institution forecloses on the property, it expects to sell the house at a profit.

The end result of all these great expectations, the home owner, also relies upon rising real estate prices. He pays the high price for the property, saddling himself in the process with large payments for principle, interest, insurance, and taxes, in the belief that the value of his home will rise. He believes he will sell it some years later, not just at the approximate amount he paid for it, thus meaning he lived in it virtually rent free, but at a higher price, making him a profit for living in it. Ever since 1945, the home buyer has demonstrated a willingness to pay ever higher prices for shelter, relying upon favorable credit from lending institutions to finance the upward spiral in real estate.

The peculiarities of the home construction and real estate industries intensify the inflationary situation. Both are dominated by a multiplicity of small firms. There are a few giants (Levitt, for example) but most homes are built by relatively small builders of a few homes or a development or two. These small builders, called contractors, deal with an even greater number of subcontractors who work on specialized parts of houses, who lay floor tile, put in windows, install heating systems, lay wiring, and perform similar tasks in home building. Beyond these types of contractors are a still larger group of businessmen involved in improvements of older homes, such as installing new siding, building recreation

rooms, renovating kitchens and bathrooms, converting single family dwellings into apartments, improving landscaping and much
more.

Unlike many industries dominated by a few large companies or
even a giant corporation, the home building business is character-
ized by small, independent concerns. As such, it is a model for the
American ideal of free enterprise. Virtually any hard-working individual can go into the home building business as a contractor or
subcontractor and usually make money.

For the most part, these small home builders must deal with the
craft labor unions, such as plumbers, bricklayers, and carpenters,
which are among the oldest, most powerful, and entrenched labor
unions. They are organized on local, district, regional, and national bases. They are well financed and their power reaches into
the highest levels of government.

The construction-craft unions have long engaged in actions
which make their members among the highest paid of any form of
unionized labor. (Probably only airline pilots are higher paid.)
They are able to control the size of their membership by enforcing
the rules of apprenticeship, by which membership is gained. The
unions have not only been able to keep out blacks and other mi-
norities in large numbers, but they have been able to keep the total
membership small. With the number of available men limited, the
unions have been able to force their wages up. It is a simple
application of the law of supply and demand. With the demand for
houses great and the supply of labor small, higher prices have
resulted.

This process has been abetted by the application of political
power by the unions. By offering or withholding financial and
other forms of political support, the craft unions have persuaded
federal, state, and local legislators to require that only union labor
be used on any governmentally-financed construction projects.
They have also encouraged high levels of government spending for

highways, dams, buildings, and other public works projects. This has kept large numbers of union members at work and resulted in relative shortages of members available for private, home building projects.

The unions have used the strike with devastating effects. The contractors, mostly small and under-financed, are unable to withstand even a short work stoppage. On public projects, contractors are required to post a performance bond that the work will be completed on time; a delaying strike can lead to financial ruination. A similar situation exists among home builders who have borrowed heavily and must depend on quick construction and early sale to remain solvent. The mere threat of a strike can throw small contractors into a panic.

The unions have also used a "see-saw" technique, striking one or a few contractors and forcing wage increases, which other contractors must accept or, in turn, be faced with a strike. The jurisdictional strike is still another weapon. The various craft unions quarrel over who is to perform a particular function in the building process. They strike until a dispute is settled, even though wages are not an issue. The effect is to force the contractor to surrender to the demands of both unions. Sometimes the contractor employs two types of workmen to do the same job, paying both high wages.

The unions have also used their power to enforce elaborate work restrictions, called "featherbedding." Only so many bricks may be laid in a day; only hand tools are used instead of power equipment. These "make work" rules drive up the costs.

The end result of all this has been twofold. The small contractors, faced with union power, have virtually surrendered to union demands. The common situation is for the unions to state what they wish their members to be paid and the contractors agree. Little or no collective bargaining occurs. The contractors simply add the labor costs to the price of the dwelling, thus forcing prices up. The second result is shoddy workmanship. The contractors, their profits squeezed, pass on the squeeze to subcontractors. The result is elaborate cost cutting through use of inferior materials and the least possible amount of labor. I once moved into a new house where the subcontractor had laid the kitchen tile over bottle caps, nails, and sawdust rather than go to the expense of sweeping the sub-flooring.

The justification for high wages in construction has been the variables of the business. Construction is outdoor work with the hazards of climate. Much of the work on large buildings is done aloft and is more hazardous. Also, when any given project is completed, the workman endures a period of unemployment until he goes to work on a new project. He may have to move his family a considerable distance to the new job, or live away from home. The craft worker believes these risks and greater expenses warrant the higher wages than are paid in more secure factory jobs. They argue that in the course of the year, their average earnings compare with those of production workers.

Be that as it may, the effect of the high wages in construction is to drive up the price of a home, but it is an error to single out the unions for blame. Profiteering takes on the characteristics of a way of life throughout the construction industry. Reforestation has been practiced in the United States for decades, yet the cost of lumber for houses has been rising for years. Just why this is so is a mystery that has defied rational explanation. Almost everything that goes into a house, it would seem, from a few petunias for a flower bed to major repairs on the roof bears a high price. More to the point, most contractors, supposedly suffering under the demands of monolithic labor unions, are able to turn a handsome profit. In midsummer, 1971, the *Miami Herald* ran a series of articles about a housing development in Dade County, Florida which it called an "instant slum." The newspaper estimated that the new houses, costing between $21,000 and $24,000, turned a profit of from

$5,000 to $7,000 each for the builder. According to the newspaper the entire development was an exercise in shoddy workmanship and was passing on the grief to unsuspecting owners.

Housing costs are driven upwards, too, by land speculation. The United States has a great deal of land, but it is not of equal value. By choice or necessity, America has an urban population. People live in or near a city because that is where the jobs are; employers locate where the employees and customers are. However circular the reasoning, America is 70 percent urban. Undeveloped and usable land in urban areas is scarce and getting scarcer. It commands astronomical prices of many thousands of dollars an acre. If held on to, it only increases in value.

The essence of profitable speculation in the United States is to buy some acreage near a city and hold on to it, paying low taxes on it as farmland. Then, as the suburbs expand and new highways are built, the land is sold at the highest possible price for a housing development. It pays even better not to sell the land but to hold on to it and lease it to the builder. Many family fortunes, reaching back many generations, rest on this principle. Consider only the present value of an acre of land in midtown Manhattan, Chicago, Detroit, or San Francisco.

The cost of land dictates the price of the house. In Fairfield County, Connecticut, north of New York City, an acre of land may cost $25,000 or more. The simplest house built upon it will thus cost $50,000. To reduce the unit land costs and increase the profits, builders try to increase the density of the population—four houses to an acre on small lots, eight garden apartments or condominiums, twenty-five or fifty or hundreds of apartments in high-rise buildings. Thus, we return again to supply and demand. The supply of land in urban areas is severely limited and shrinking all the time. Here, where the demand is high, land costs can be astronomical. Builders—and eventually individual owners or renters—are forced to absorb the high price that results.

Housing costs are also driven upwards through a variety of legal and institutional devices supposedly aimed at protecting the home buyer and/or the lending institution. All are lumped under the term *closing costs*. These include title searches to insure that the deed is properly registered and that there are no other claims against the property, attorneys' fees for making such searches, and insurance against future claims against the title. In addition, local governments collect various payments called transfer taxes, usually 1 percent or more of the selling price of the property.

These closing costs vary by locality. The Committee on Banking and Currency of the House of Representatives conducted an investigation into closing costs in February, 1972. It found the costs ranged from a high of nearly 7 percent of the value of the property in Montgomery and Prince George Counties, Maryland, adjacent to Washington, D.C., to less than 2 percent in the Boston, Massachusetts, area. The closing costs, paid in cash at the time the house is purchased, normally run between several hundred to nearly two thousand dollars on a house costing $20,000. More than a few unsuspecting home buyers, having scraped together the down payment on a house, have found themselves further indebted to meet usurious closing costs. The House committee sharply questioned the need for many of these closing costs, citing their chief value as enrichment of lending institutions, title insurance companies, and lawyers.

Another widespread practice which afflicts the less than affluent home buyer is the "point" system, a point being 1 percent of the value of the house. Because Veterans or FHA mortgages, insured by the federal government, bear a lower rate of interest than conventional bank or savings and loan mortgages, the lenders sometimes make up the difference by demanding points in cash at the time of purchase. There are also instances in which the builder or real estate agent has demanded points. These are sometimes disguised as "services by the lender" or whomever. Such practices drive up housing costs.

Finally, a variety of local laws increase costs. The zoning laws, building codes, and building inspection regulations are all designed to protect the buyer against unsafe or inferior dwellings. But in practice they are all too often a financial millstone around his neck, for if local officials are corrupt, the laws are a source of bribery and financial kickbacks, and the owner will pay for a "jerry-built" house as though it had been built properly.

The zoning laws are intended to insure that land is used appropriately for residential, commercial, or industrial uses. To give the proverbial example, zoning is intended to insure that a noisy boiler factory is not built next to homes. More likely examples would be a gasoline station or a high-rise office building in a residential area, a housing development at the end of a runway to a jet airport. The trouble with zoning is that the land use tends to be frozen in time, while neighborhoods and the desires of the residents change. Zoning laws try to provide for this change by permitting exceptions. The local zoning board can agree to put a high density apartment house in an area zoned for single family dwellings or to permit a liquor store or dry cleaning shop or other commercial enterprise because it feels the area has changed or there is need for these exceptions. Unfortunately, the board can be led to make these exemptions because of graft. Sometimes board members receive money under the table from builders (or lawyers representing them) because the building or factory will be very profitable.

Building codes are a notorious source of high costs. Great effort has gone into amending these codes in recent years, but there are still codes which preclude the use of modern materials, such as aluminum and poured concrete. The outdated codes do not permit use of new plumbing and electrical wiring. Most infamous are those codes which prohibit the use of power tools on building sites.

Building codes are enforced by building inspectors. These individuals come to the site during and after construction to determine that the house is built according to the code. The inspectors have immense power. They can overlook violations of the more out-moded provisions of the code or they can insist upon strict compliance. They can be prompt in appearing for inspections or they can delay the project because they fail to appear. They can create great expense by compelling work to be torn down and re-done according to the code. And frequently there is not just one inspector but a battery of them for wiring, plumbing, and other aspects of the construction. A hardly universal but all too frequent practice is for the contractor to pay off the inspector to insure his prompt arrival and his less than militant enforcement of the code. These payoffs, naturally, are added to the cost of the house.

All of these factors—and this list has hardly been exhaustive—drive up real estate prices in America. As a result, truly low-cost housing is virtually nonexistent. In the words of Mr. Finger, who began this chapter, "the average FHA-insured home, including land . . . serves a fairly high income range." We take up the repercussions of this fact next.

THE HIGH COST OF SUBURBIA

CHAPTER THREE

The great expanding balloon of housing costs in the United States has effects on American life which are both little known and little short of staggering.

Harold B. Finger, whose speech was quoted in the last chapter, also reported some statistics on the income with which American families pay for the ever more expensive housing. From 1965 through 1970, average hourly earnings rose 41 percent (though only 29 percent for manufacturing wages). Median family income rose 46 percent from approximately $7,000 to about $10,000 a year. However, with a 46 percent greater income the average American family during that period paid 67 percent more for a house, along with bearing monthly payments and property taxes that rose 85 percent each.

These, of course, are average figures and possess all the evils thereof. There are places in the United States where a $26,000 home is luxury housing and wealthy suburbs where absolutely no properties can be acquired for such an absurdly low figure. But these average figures enable us to make several statements that may help to illuminate the housing problem.

First, there is virtually no such thing as new, low cost housing in the United States. The only housing available at all for under $15,000 is a mobile home. These house-trailers are marvels of compactness and efficiency. In many ways they are ideal for older couples whose physical activities are restricted. On the other hand, they are almost impossibly small for a family, particularly with young, active children. Externally, they are monstrously ugly, and a collection of them in a trailer park is a scar upon the landscape.

Second, with few exceptions about the only housing available for under $20,000 or even $25,000 are older homes. Such relative bargains exist mainly either in rural areas with depressed housing markets (because jobs are scarce and few people want to live there); or in the central core areas of small and large cities where again jobs are scarce and the quality of life has deteriorated because of blight, overcrowding, crime, traffic, and pollution. Again, few people want it.

Third, it is now, more than ever, difficult to buy and own a home because the traditional rule of thumb is for a family to spend about two and a half times its annual income for a house. Using Mr. Finger's statistics, that is what happened in 1970. The median income per family was $10,000 and the average FHA house cost $25,000. The monthly expense for that average house was $272. All right so far. But Mr. Finger did not explain whether the median income was gross income (before payment of income taxes) or net income (after taxes). Nor did he itemize whether housing expense included property taxes and insurance, as well as mortgage payments on principle and interest. Even if the most optimistic situation is assumed—net income of $10,000 and $272 monthly payments that include taxes and insurance—the family is still paying almost 35 percent of its income for housing.

On top of this must go some spending for repairs and upkeep of the property (a mower for that crabgrass) and the expenses for heating, electricity, sewage and garbage services, as well as telephone service. Under the best of circumstances these items must come to several hundred dollars a year. And, since no one can live in an empty house, further outlays of thousands of dollars must be made for furniture, appliances, television, and their upkeep.

Clearly, based on government statistics, the average family buying an average house in 1970 spent at least 40 percent and probably closer to half its income on owning, operating, and living in a place of shelter. If that family's income went down or it splurged on a larger house and more expensive furnishing, its expenditures for shelter could easily exceed half the family income.

There is more. That typical house is probably located in a typical suburb somewhere, which means a nearly total absence of public transportation. The family must own a car, which is an indirect housing expense. The car will cost from several hundred dollars for a vintage vehicle to several thousand dollars for a new one. The expense of operating either one will be several hundred dollars a year at a minimum.

A closer look at some of the intricacies of home ownership will indicate just how large an investment an American makes in his home. The government-insured Veterans and FHA loans, while still available and used, are being replaced by a form of conventional mortgage loan. Banks and other lending institutions will lend up to 90 percent of the appraised value of the home being purchased. In actual practice the bank will lend only 80 percent of the value, meaning the buyer-borrower must put up 20 percent in cash. If the full 90 percent is to be borrowed, the lending institution will require the purchase of mortgage insurance from a private company. The biggest insuring company is the Mortgage Guarantee Insurance Corporation (MGIC).

The borrower is required to pay 1 percent of the original mortgage in cash at the time of settlement—$200 on a $20,000 mortgage. Half that money goes to the lender and half to the insurer. Then, the interest charges on the loan are increased by one-quarter of 1 percent. This money goes to the insurance company. In banking parlance this type of loan is called "magic," a word based upon the MGIC initials of the largest insurer.

The advantages of this type of loan are that both the lender and the insurer make money by risking the greater amount of mortgage money. Even better from their standpoint, the lender avoids all the red tape and bother of dealing with the federal government for an FHA-insured loan. The advantage to the home buyer is that his cash down payment is reduced. He does not have to delay his purchase by waiting for FHA approval of his loan. Perhaps best, the borrower can also pre-pay his principle—that is, make extra or lump sum payments—thus reducing the amount of interest he pays.

At the end of 1972, the interest charges on a conventional home mortgage was 7.5 percent and 7.75 percent on a "magic" loan. There might be some variance in these interest rates according to locality, but these rates may be considered representative. If a home buyer borrows $10,000 at the rate of 7.75 percent interest for thirty years—most of his working lifetime—he must make monthly payments on principle and interest of $71.65. Over the thirty-year life of the loan he will have paid to the lender (and insurer) $26,794—more than two and a half times what he borrowed. The following table projects these figures for large loans more typically needed for home purchases:

Amount Borrowed	Monthly Payment	Amount Repaid
$20,000	$143.30	$53,588
$30,000	$214.95	$80,382
$40,000	$286.60	$107,176

The effect of these figures is that if a family bought an extremely small, modest home in late 1972 or early 1973 for $22,000, made a 10 percent down payment of $2,000 and borrowed the remaining $20,000 under the above loan arrangement, the family is really paying $53,588 plus the original $2,000 for a total of $55,588 for the dwelling. The purchaser can reduce the total amount by borrowing the money for only twenty or twenty-five years, but the monthly payments increase sharply because of faster payments on principle.

It may be seen, then, that even the most modest of homes is a tremendous investment. One thinks of a $55,000 home as a quite luxurious dwelling, when in fact what is bought for that eventual sum is a most minimal habitat, probably an older home in a rural area or in a declining neighborhood of a central city.

The real shocker is that the $55,000 is still not enough. To be realistic, the buyer must add taxes and fire insurance on the property—another $10,000 to $20,000 over the thirty-year period.*

The high cost of a house (one is again tempted to use the word astronomical) and the fact that approximately half the family income ** is used to pay for owning and living in it, leads to the question: how do Americans do it?

The answer is that a significant number of more fortunate Americans find ways to reduce the cost of shelter. The age of the person can be an asset. If he is old enough to have purchased a home in the late 1940's, the 1950's, or early 1960's, he probably was able to pay considerably less for it and to have borrowed money at a lower rate of interest. If he and his family have continued to live in that house and his income rose, his costs of shelter are considerably less. One bank official whom I interviewed has done precisely this. He estimated his housing costs at about 25 percent of his income.

Buyers who bought their house twenty or so years ago have been able to take advantage of rising real estate prices. They purchased a succession of ever larger homes, selling each at a profit, which was re-invested in the more expensive dwelling.

* The preceding discussion and statistical table were prepared at the beginning of 1973 when interest rates ranged from 7 to 7.5 percent. Within a few months interest rates for home mortgages rose to 9 and 9.5 percent as part of the Nixon administration's efforts to curb inflation. The higher interest rates, combined with a shortage of credit for home mortgages, had the effect of reducing housing construction and real estate transactions. The figures presented in the preceding discussion will undoubtedly be inaccurate as interest rates go up or down. The figures presented here are to be taken as representative of the high cost of interest payments when a home is purchased.

** This estimate, which I have verified with a number of mortgage bankers, was based on a median take-home income of $10,000. The same would probably be true for higher income people. A man taking home $20,000 a year and living in a $50,000 home (two and one-half times his income) would probably spend half or more of his income buying and maintaining such a large home. Perhaps this estimate of half the income for shelter in the form of a new house would be reduced only in the case of large incomes of over $50,000 a year. Even then a less opulent life style would be required.

The Elysian Fields of home ownership in America is for a couple to have purchased a comfortable home when they were in their early twenties and, at considerable sacrifice, to have patiently made their mortgage payments for twenty-five or thirty years. If the house and the neighborhood have not depreciated, the family owns the house clear of debt when the breadwinner is in his fifties, usually a time of peak earnings. He continues to live in the house rent free until his retirement at age sixty-five. He and his wife sell the property at a profit and use the money to finance a leisurely, well-deserved retirement. Or the couple continues to live in the house at low cost until death, leaving it as a legacy to their children.

This home ownership dream comes true a significant but unknown percentage of the time. But for others the dream can be shattered by deterioration of the home or the neighborhood which slashes the value of the house. Or the couple's retirement income is insufficient to meet the taxes, upkeep, and utilities on the home. All their patience and payments have come to nought.

The accident of age is of utmost importance in home ownership in America. It may safely be said that couples now in their forties and fifties never had it so good. In the 1950's, when these couples were just beginning married life, representative earnings were from $4,000 to $7,000 a year. Brand new houses were available in suburban developments for $10–$12,000. More commodious split levels went for from $15,000 to $18,000. A $20,000 house meant you were in a higher income bracket. The lowest-price houses required a down payment of $1,000 or less, and some financial arrangements even called for nothing down. The home was financed through a Veterans loan at 4 or 4.5 percent interest or a FHA loan at 5 or 5.5 percent. Taxes were low. A common experience was to make monthly payments on the lower-price homes of $90 to $100 a month, including principle, interest, insurance, and taxes.

In home ownership, those were the good old days. The unspendable savings accumulated during World War II combined with easy credit to create a tremendous home construction boom. Suburban developments sprang up by the millions, seemingly overnight. Within a few short years, the nation was transformed from one in which two-thirds of the families were renters to a country in which two-thirds were home owners. The vast exodus to the suburbs ushered in superhighways, shopping malls, suburban sprawl, and a host of other benefits and ills, of which more in pages to come.

Consider the young couple in their twenties today. Representative earnings for the breadwinner are from $6,000 to $9,000. Chances are that he will not find any new house in the suburbs of most American cities for less than $25,000, and he may be extremely fortunate to find one at that price. He probably will end up paying $20,000 or so for one of those generation-old houses that originally sold for $10,000—and find it needs a new roof, furnace, and other major repairs. The young couple will find they need a down payment of $2,000 or more, certainly when closing costs are included. They will pay a good deal more than 4 or 5 percent interest. Taxes, insurance, and utilities have gone up. Payments of $100 a month are a mere echo from halcyon days. The couple will be lucky to get off for twice that amount. One home owner in an East Coast suburb, while gratified at the increased value of his home he bought five years previously, remarked, "I couldn't afford to buy my own house today." His is perhaps a common situation.

I asked a number of bank officials how young couples manage to buy homes today. The consensus was: "with difficulty." A common method, the bankers said, was for the couple to have help from their parents who provide the down payment on the house as an out-and-out gift or as a long-term, interest-free loan. In the latter event, the parents are providing a free second mortgage. In some cases, the parents mortgage their own home to provide for the newlyweds.

Another common method is for the couple to live as cheaply as possible in a small rented apartment and postpone having children while both of them work. Gradually they are able to save the down payment. Not uncommonly both continue to work after moving into their own home, just to meet the house payments. One lending official admitted more seriously than in jest that perhaps the high cost of housing had more to do with the nation's low birthrate than the oral contraceptive pill.*

The high cost of shelter and related automotive transportation in the United States is having a tremendous effect on the quality of American life. With these two taking half or more of the spendable income of the average family, relatively less money is available for food, clothing, medical care, education, travel, recreation, and cultural activities.

This unbalanced kind of budget has some other effects on American family life. For all but a minority of Americans, the maintenance of a family income of $10,000 or more means that the wife and mother must work full or part time. Many women enjoy career woman status, but polls have shown that most women work because they have to, rather than because they want to. When there are young children in the home, the absence of at least one parent from the home as the youngsters go to and from school and other activities can lead to emotional and disciplinary difficulties. Some deterioration of family unity is a virtual certainty.

---

* The postponement of children while a home and other possessions are accumulated is a major change from the practices of the 1950's. Easier home acquisition made it possible for couples to start a family at an earlier age. If indeed the postponement of children is becoming an American phenomenon, we will be emulating other cultures. In Spain, where I lived for several years, it is customary for couples to become engaged in their late teens. Marriage is postponed for ten or twelve years, while both work and save, gradually accumulating the money for a house or apartment and its furnishings. When all is paid for, the couple marry in their late twenties. This custom results from the great difficulty in obtaining consumer credit for installment payments. It has the effect of keeping the birthrate low in a Catholic nation.

It is perhaps far from universal, but in some families the purpose of family life becomes more the earning of money, the payment of bills, and the acquisition of possessions, than the enjoyment of life and its blessings. One banker, sympathetic to the plight of home owners, said, "I think people have the feeling today that they are not getting ahead, but slowly sliding backwards."

Before leaving this discussion of the housing problems of the successful, solvent portion of the population, there might be some wisdom in pondering a possible future event—the unthinkable, unspeakable bursting of that great inflationary balloon of housing prices. The pinprick could come from such economic factors as runaway inflation, unemployment, high interest rates and a shortage of money, reduced foreign trade, shortages of oil,* or a combination of any of these economic happenings. However the federal government, through manipulation of the economy, has powerful weapons with which to combat these factors.

The great intangible pinprick which government would find it difficult to combat would be buyer resistance to the high prices. If large numbers of Americans should independently decide that the value of that house in the greensward isn't worth the price of half their income and refused to pay it—or prices rose so high they were unable to pay it—the result could be a sharp drop in real estate prices, a bursting of that huge balloon, mass foreclosures, and an unspeakable economic depression engulfing the world. Banking officials whom I questioned privately about this replied, with just a

---

* This paragraph was written in early 1973 before the nation encountered a fuel shortage, or the so-called "energy crisis," in which the United States sustained shortages of crude oil, oil products such as gasoline, coal, natural gas, and other fuels necessary for transportation, heating, and electric power. In trying to think of factors or situations that could deflate the housing market, it seemed likely that a fuel shortage might be one of them. Indeed, the fuel shortage did coincide with a sharp drop in the number of new homes under construction. Many factors were involved, however, and these are discussed throughout this book.

little hesitation, "It hasn't happened yet. Real estate prices have been going up since 1945." It is fervently to be hoped such optimism is justified.

This discussion of the monetary problems of home ownership has been based on the fact that the *median* income of American families in 1970 was $10,000 annually. Median means in the middle. Allowing for those families whose income is exactly in the middle, it may be stated that nearly half the families earn more than $10,000 a year and an equal number less than $10,000. The difficulties discussed up to now have applied to those earning $10,000 or more. We must now take up the housing problems of the half of the population which earn less than $10,000.

THE PROBLEMS OF POVERTY

CHAPTER FOUR

Millions of Americans do not make enough money to afford any but the cheapest, most rundown housing.

The people of the United States first became aware of the poverty among our relative plenty with the publication of the book *The Other America* by Michael Harrington in 1963. The following year President Lyndon B. Johnson launched the "War on Poverty," hoping to abolish it in this land within a generation.

The first task was to define poverty. Government experts computed the cost of the bare essentials needed to sustain life and, based on 1963 prices, decided that any family of four earning less than $3,000 a year was indigent, suffering from poverty. That figure has been adjusted upwards as prices rose through the years until in 1971 the poverty level was $4,000 or less for a four-member family.

The appalling fact is that there are families who somehow survive on that low amount, when more recent government computations show that a more realistic poverty line for a family of four is almost $8,000.* Since 1967 the Bureau of Labor Statistics has figured the lower, middle, and upper income needs of four-member families living in urban settings. The figures were based on the actual prices of essential and realistic items in a family budget; that is, how families actually live rather than how they perhaps ought to live. For the record, the upper income family of four in New York City spent at least $19,238 in 1971 and the middle income family at least $12,585. The expenses of a lower income family was figured at $7,578. All of these incomes are gross, that is, total earnings before taxes.

That figure of $7,578 is a long way from the "official" poverty

* Some of the statistics in this chapter were derived from the provocative article "Crisis of the *Under*employed—In Much of the Inner City 60 Percent Don't Earn Enough for a Decent Standard of Living" by William Spring, Bennett Harrison, and Thomas Vietorisz in the November 5, 1972, issue of *The New York Times Magazine*.

line of $4,000. It may be argued that New York City is a higher priced place to live than other cities. It is, but not very much. In 1970, the national urban average for lower income families was $6,960 when the New York City figure was $7,183.

How is that money spent? A breakdown of the $7,183 required in New York City in 1970 is as follows.

* Federal, state, and local taxes took $28.65 a week or $1,490 a year.

* For $100 a month or $1,200 a year the family of four rented the cheapest possible apartment, described as only barely inhabitable.

* Another $15 a month or $183 a year went for cleaning supplies, curtains, furniture repairs, and the like. The statistics assume the family somehow possesses furniture and appliances without suggesting how they were acquired.

* Food consumes $40.20 a week or $2,091 a year. That does not qualify as eating high on the proverbial hog for four people.

* Another $433 a year or $8.32 a week was figured for transportation. This included the cost of necessary public transportation plus the cost of buying and operating a six-year-old automobile.

* Medical expenses of $15.59 a week or $811 a year.

* Life insurance premiums and charitable contributions came to $6.88 a week or $347 a year.

* A final $7.25 a week or $377 a year went for such familiar pleasures as television, movies, radios, tobacco, and recreation.*

These monthly or weekly expenditures vary up or down, but average out at these levels for a year.

These figures describe a rather spartan existence without much

---

* This breakdown was reported in the Spring-Harrison-Vietorisz article. In one of those nightmarish errors that plague writers, the figures add up to only $6,932 a year instead of $7,183. I assumed that the missing $251 a year goes for a necessity of life omitted from this compilation—clothing; later, in a telephone conversation, one of the authors concurred with this assumption.

leeway for luxury, error, folly, ill health, or bad luck. In fact the figures are rather unbelievable. If a family could buy, license, insure, and maintain a six-year-old car for $433 a year, they certainly didn't drive it very much. We may state with positive assurance that there is no way such a family will purchase a home or apartment without a large government subsidy. And, if that subsidy is provided and the family moves into its own home, there is no way it can afford the utilities, maintenance, and other expenses of home ownership.

The shocking fact about the $7,183 on which this family of four lived in 1970 is that it represented the earnings of a fairly skilled, fully employed workman. If a man or woman works forty hours a week, fifty-two weeks a year and is paid $3.50 an hour, he will have earned $7,280 a year.

That simple fact begins to strike at the heart of America's poverty and thus housing problem. A man earning $3.50 an hour or $140 a week in America's urban areas, where 70 percent of Americans live, can support himself, his wife, and two children at a level only slightly above sheer subsistence.

The depth of the problem, as reported by Spring, Harrison, and Vietorisz and based upon government statistics, is that perhaps 60 percent of the people living in the inner cities of America do not earn that $7,000 a year which will maintain a borderline "decent standard of living." Fully 30 percent of these inner city dwellers do not even reach the official $4,000 poverty level. These figures are based on surveys of fifty-one urban areas where thirteen million people live, 49.5 percent of them black, 47.9 percent white (including 11.8 percent of Spanish-speaking origins), and 2.6 percent other racial or ethnic origins. These difficult financial straits affected approximately one-third of the total population of the cities surveyed.

It is precisely in these downtrodden inner cities where the nation's serious housing problem exists, with blight, overcrowding, deterioration, crime, addiction, and all the rest. It is here that, in Mr. Romney's view, the nation has wasted $100 billion.

In my opinion, that 60 percent figure is the most shocking statistic I have ever encountered in a long professional experience with shocking statistics. It was arrived at by adding together estimates of those people who are unemployed but actively looking for jobs; those who have given up in discouragement at ever finding work; those who can find only part time or temporary jobs; and those large numbers of people who work full time yet are unable to earn that base figure of $7,000 for a four-person family.

To grasp the difficulties involved in urban life, $3.50 an hour, $140 a week, $7,000 a year is more than twice the minimum wage. Sixty percent of the manufacturing plants in New York City have median wages of less than $3.50 an hour, that is, half their employees earn less than that amount. These are wages paid to rather skilled people, such as maintenance carpenters or sheet metal workers in factories, machinery operators, bartenders (with tips), full charge bookkeepers, top retail sales people. With the exception of laborers in the high paid construction industry, unskilled and semi-skilled workers do not earn over $3.50 per hour.*

It might be argued that the family income could be increased if the wife or another member worked. This is the typical family situation in America, with 1.7 members employed in the average family. But among the low-income residents of cities, the average employment is 0.7 persons per family. There is not enough work for even one member of an average family to find a full time job.

---

* These job categories were supplied by the Connecticut State Employment Service in Bridgeport. Wages may vary up or down in other localities. Bridgeport is considered an economically depressed area. Economist Bennett Harrison of the Massachusetts Institute of Technology points out that state employment service wage figures are often distorted. Only low paying employers customarily use the state services. Higher paying employers tend to obtain workers through private means. In any event, wages of $3.50 an hour are paid to rather skilled and experienced workers.

There are many factors which create a slum, but one of them, obviously, is poverty, a peculiar type of poverty. Laziness, bad judgment, folly, drunkenness, disease, bad luck—all of which fit the popular stereotype of the poor—are undoubtedly causes of poverty. But it is now known that a man can work full time at a job requiring skill and experience, applying great discipline to himself and his expenditures, and still be unable to rise out of a condition of indigence.

Public officials and scholars are just now beginning to grasp the fact that simply having a job and working does not solve the poverty problem in present-day America.

Hard work for low wages (sometimes at more than one job) is a common experience for the poor and near poor in America. It is an aberrated form of the American dream that efforts to earn seven and even eight thousand dollars a year produce only the minimum of food, shelter, and clothing and leave scant hope for a home in suburbia and a comfortable old age. What is remarkable is that so many of the poor and near poor (perhaps a majority of them, perhaps not, for no one knows for certain) continue to work and struggle and hope for the future at all.

More affluent Americans perhaps have difficulty realizing what it means to teeter constantly on the edge of poverty. A family's hard won gains are easily wiped out by a loss of a job, a lay off, a strike, illness or accidents, dental bills, major repairs to the car, stove, or refrigerator. Such normally happy events as Christmas and birthdays are dampened by the financial sacrifices the parents must make to provide the children with only a fraction of the gifts they want.

Of course poverty has been much written about, often romantically. Rising from poverty through hard work was a staple of fiction in this country. And poverty was a fact—privation was the common experience in the 1930's, and Americans now in their 40's and 50's vividly recall those difficult days, as well as their families' rise in fortunes. The question is to what extent this "pulling yourself up by your bootstraps" is possible today. The younger person just starting out on a career and earning low wages or the older person stuck at low pay because of the limitations of his skills faces a difficult task in improving his standard of living. He must pay high prices with low earnings. Food, clothing, transportation consume large portions of his budget. That dream house in suburbia becomes more distant and for many utterly impossible. There is relatively little use in exhorting the poor and near poor to work, for perhaps half the available jobs do not pay enough to lift them out of poverty. Their only hope is to find ways to upgrade their skills so they can earn more money. In center-cities and economically depressed areas this is easier said than done.

Nor does it help the poor and near poor to suggest to them that they are better off than the starving, homeless peasants of India or even many of the working classes in England and the rest of Western Europe. The United States is not India or even England. The distances between Harlem and Fifth Avenue, Hough and Shaker Heights, Watts and Beverly Hills are not great. Nor does the less affluent American need to travel at all to know that he is poor. He merely has to flick on his television set to see inconceivable luxuries portrayed as necessities of life. The good life, the great society, it would seem, are embodied in pop-up French toast, dry underarms, platform soles on shoes, and a mouthwash that tastes bad. Life seemingly cannot go on without bucket seats and electric toothbrushes. The poor and near poor see and want the glittering baubles of America even more perhaps than those who can afford them.

There are ways to obtain the necessary luxuries and many of the poor are experts at these tasks. From a viewpoint of ivory-tower ethics, the methods involve a bit of fraud. From a standpoint of poverty, the measures take on an aura of simple wisdom.

In the inner city, the general term is "hustling," which means making a few dollars on the side. Some representative examples are using your car to drive a few passengers to their destination, being better at playing pool or cards than other people, offering an evening's companionship to a male in return for a few gifts, selling items the ownership of which is in doubt, assisting people who wish to bet a little money on the numbers or the results of a sports event. All of these methods of earning money are illegal, but they are so frequently done that the justification for the illegality becomes rather obscure.

The nation's entire welfare system invites fraud. The few dollars earned by honest employment, such as a temporary or part time job, can easily be concealed from the Welfare Department. It is much easier still to conceal the earnings from a little illegal hustling. Under the welfare laws of most states, a woman cannot collect welfare unless she is abandoned by her husband. It is rather simple for the man to pretend to leave the home, while the woman offers a false trail to the police as to his whereabouts.

The nation's credit system offers a method for obtaining luxuries. Cars, appliances, and television sets are bought on the installment plan. A few payments are made while the purchases are used and enjoyed. This time can be extended by such ruses as partial payments and tearful promises—or simply not being at home when the men come to repossess the items. But repossessed they soon are, then re-sold to another family which also buys them on time. Durable items may be re-sold several times. Dealers and lending institutions make a great deal of money on the process. The poor lose money, but have the temporary, at least, use of the coveted luxuries. It's better than nothing—which is all they can legitimately afford.

Hustling, welfare fraud, and abuse of credit are either illegal or unethical. Moralists and government leaders bemoan them, but to many Americans teetering on the edge of poverty they are necessary to make life anything more than constant drudgery. And it does not befit many of our more affluent citizens to take too high a moral tone—such practices of the very poor are easily equated with the tax havens, tax evasions, credit excesses, and bankruptcy laws used by the affluent citizen.

More serious are the temptations of the poor to engage in open crime—shoplifting, larceny from a cash register ("tilltapping"), purse snatching, pocketpicking, mugging, burglary, armed robbery, and worse. Or to escape a dreary, frustrating life of despair through alcohol or drug addiction, engaging in crime and drug pushing to finance the excesses.

Poverty breeds poverty all over the world. To escape it requires tremendous amounts of intelligence, hard work, perseverence, discipline, courage, pride, and luck—and even given all that, there is no assurance these qualities will enable a person to make it today.

This brief discussion of poverty is wholly germane to this book, for there is a direct relationship between poverty and housing. When an income of seven or eight thousand dollars a year relegates a family of four to the most minimal housing in an inner city, what can be available to those earning less—flats with inadequate heat, cold water, garbage strewn in the stairways, and infestations of rats and cockroaches. Such buildings may be structurally sound, in more loving and wealthy hands they might even be beautiful, but because of poverty, the buildings are overcrowded. Maintenance is minimal at best. If not worn out, the buildings are deteriorating rapidly. There is nothing about them to inspire pride of ownership or pleasure in occupancy. Almost everything that happens to them leads to further deterioration and their subsequent occupancy by ever poorer tenants.

As the buildings go, so do the neighborhoods in a cycle of poorer residents, reduced opportunities for employment, less prosperous stores, then higher crime, addiction, and disease rates. The stable, ambitious, caring people leave the neighborhood, although there are many such people who are simply trapped in neighborhoods which have deteriorated into pestholes.

There are many causes for the housing problem. One of them is widespread poverty that ruins buildings, degenerates neighborhoods, detracts from the quality of life, and leads to a struggle involving various forms of immorality, dishonesty, and escape through drugs. In the end, much of that which enobles and distinguishes men and women is lost; they become less than human.

THE URBAN CRISIS AND HOW IT GREW

CHAPTER FIVE

America's housing problem did not occur overnight. It has been a long time abuilding. Its roots might well be traced back over a century to the industrialization of America. But for more practical purposes, we need only look to the last thirty years or so.

The Great Depression, which began with the stock market crash in 1929, was perhaps not the worst in history in terms of human suffering, but it surely was the longest. It lasted in various degrees of severity until the United States entered World War II in December, 1941. During most of those years, there was high unemployment, with up to one quarter of the work force jobless. Those who did work had their wages sharply cut. The savings of large numbers of people were wiped out in the widespread bank failures. In a word, there was a tremendous shortage of money. Most important to this discussion is the fact that for more than a decade virtually no new private housing was built and very little maintenance and repair was done.

Beginning in the mid-1930's, the nation launched a program of federally-financed public housing projects. They served two purposes. They offered shelter for the poor and unemployed who had been driven from their homes during the economic hard times. Even better, the projects stimulated the depressed economy. Workmen were employed, materials ordered, utilities installed, furnishings purchased. It was recognized even then that housing had a large "spin off" into the entire economy, stimulating manufacture and sale of many products other than houses.

Public housing helped pull the nation out of the depression, although it was only a small part of the total effort. Still, the very success of these early housing efforts is a curse today. The housing was looked upon as temporary. The poor, like everyone else in those days, were viewed as simply "down on their luck." They simply needed a little help until prosperity returned with plentiful jobs and money. So the early public housing was built to provide only the essentials of subsistence. Such unnecessary accoutrements as interior doors to closets and cupboards or extra electrical connections were eliminated. Exteriors and interiors were uniformly dreary. Unfortunately, all the early public housing structures were built exceedingly well. Many of them are still standing and have had to undergo extensive and expensive remodeling to make them even halfway decent places to live.

The depression was followed by World War II. As part of the all-out effort, an immense amount of wartime housing was built for workers in defense plants. This housing, again publicly financed, was built with extreme rapidity. Construction was flimsy and again the barest essentials for living were provided. No one minded, for living in such quarters was a small sacrifice compared to that being made by the fighting men at the various war fronts. But much of this housing has had to be remodeled or replaced.

It is important to keep in mind that public housing by war's end in 1945 was only a fraction of the total national housing. What had happened to the older, private housing? It had been almost totally neglected during fifteen years of depression and total war. There was no money in the depression nor materials and labor during the war to perform any but the most essential maintenance on homes and apartments. The once elegant urban housing which, with normal care, might have withstood the effects of aging, deteriorated rapidly under the onslaught of unavoidable neglect and the overcrowding caused by the war effort.

No particular clairvoyance was needed in 1945 to see that the nation faced a housing crisis. About twelve million men and women were to be mustered out of the armed services to make a belated start on careers and family life. They would be seeking housing in a market that was already in short supply. There was a virtual absence of new, decent housing. Many millions of housing units were needed—and overnight would hardly be quick enough.

The federal government, from President Harry S Truman to freshmen congressmen, recognized the problem. A step was taken which in hindsight can only be called pure genius. It not only solved the problem but changed the face of America forever and, by extension, the rest of the world. Unfortunately, a host of problems resulted which have yet to be fully understood, let alone solved.

Uncle Sam performed a revolution in financing. The federal government *insured* loans. Through VA and FHA loans, the United States Government simply took the risk out of home mortgages. In an instant, the federal government said to lending institutions, in effect, "Lend money to almost anyone to buy a house. The good faith, credit, and tax resources of the federal government stand behind this person. If he cannot repay his loan, the government will." With a flourish of a presidential pen, all the risk went out of home financing. Billions of dollars of private capital were made available for home construction.

Homes were built by the millions. "Developments" and "subdivisions," as they were called, were measured in the thousands of units, not hundreds; in square miles, not acres. Farmland was transformed into suburbia. We became a nation of home owners.

The effects of VA and FHA home financing are staggering. The housing boom, which this financing fostered, is the root cause of America's prolonged prosperity, its life-style, and many of the really serious problems the nation faces today.

Tens of millions of Americans, on the order of a third to a half of the population, moved to the suburbs within a very few years. It was one of (if not *the*) greatest human migration in history. These people moved into what had been virtually empty land. Everything had to be provided—houses, lawns, roads, stores, schools, churches, utilities—in a word, entire communities. The simple construction of the houses made millions of jobs. Then millions more jobs were made for all the people supplying the materials for those houses—lumberjacks, sawmill operators, brick and cement makers, glass makers, and all the rest. Those millions of houses needed furnaces and water pipe and shingles for the roof and furniture and appliances and more appliances and electricity to run the appliances and more and more—and more.

Above all else the suburbanite needed an automobile.* He and his family were on the new frontier, isolated from employment. His simple existence depended upon a set of wheels. And, since many of the housing developments were so physically large and so isolated—many were built without sidewalks—it was necessary to drive to the supermarket or shopping center (both essentially postwar phenomena) for the sustenance of life. Evening shopping became a new American custom.

A second car then became almost essential to permit the stay-at-home wife to shop, make visits to the doctor and dentist, and simply to squire the kids around to their friends and activities. Because suburbia is a vast cultural wasteland and there isn't very much to do at best, teenagers came to feel compelled to drive a car upon reaching age sixteen. Not to have a car or a friend who had a car was to be bored and lonely. Thus, the American family became a two-car family—or three or four or five.

The automotive industry is the largest in the United States. Just ponder what the manufacture and sale of ten million new cars a year means in terms of automotive assembly and production of steel, glass, rubber, oil, gasoline, leather, fabrics, wire, and a hundred other basic products. Consider all the service stations and repair shops. And, all those cars need something to drive on so as a result we have streets and roads and superhighways—and superhighways on top of superhighways. And, all those cars need to

---

* We could get into a very large chicken-and-egg discussion of whether the house fostered the car or the car led to the suburban house. It is certainly true that most Americans couldn't have gone house hunting in suburbia without a car. But it is also true that the house could not have been lived in without a car to get to and from work. It is probably best to say that the two go together like the proverbial birds of a feather. Chickens lay eggs and those eggs become chickens.

have places to go, so we have new factories, shopping centers, drive-in restaurants and drive-in everything else, along with drive-in banks to pay for it all. And, when the cars are not being driven they have to be parked. The value of private garages, public parking garages, and black-topped parking lots in the United States probably exceeds the gross national product of 90 percent of the nations of the earth.

The housing revolution that moved the nation to suburbia and led to the automobile for transportation depended on one other thing—communication to alleviate the isolation which Americans had gone to such great expense to achieve. The communication came in two forms, the telephone and television. Suburban Americans wanted to stay in touch with their fellow man and be entertained.*

The housing-transportation-communication revolution begot by VA and FHA financing has been a remarkable financial success. Only a miniscule proportion of all those millions of federally-insured loans had to be foreclosed. The FHA has been a money maker in this area of its activities. Indeed, the idea of insuring loans has been so financially successful that, as we have seen, private insurance companies have entered the business for profit.

The fantastic migration of Americans to the suburbs was accompanied by a second immense migration, that of black people northward from the South. It began in 1917 with World War I and accelerated, reaching a peak in the 1950's and 1960's. The 11 percent black minority of America was transformed from a largely rural Southern population to a predominantly urban Northern pop-

---

* There are many who will quarrel with this analysis of contemporary America which traces its origins to VA and FHA financing. One could trace the transformation of America through the threads of transportation or communication. The internal combustion engine and the transistor surely rank among the more profound (or devilish, from another point of view) inventions in the history of the world. In any event, I believe we must search for and control these root causes, if our problems are to be solved.

ulation. There was also a movement of Spanish-speaking Mexican-Americans and Puerto Ricans to cities.

The Negroes moved into the dwellings which had been vacated by the whites who moved to suburbia. There they joined a sizeable group of people who had not joined the suburban exodus for a variety of reasons. They were the black middle classes (denied access to suburbia because of prejudice), the elderly (too old to get financing), people tied to old neighborhoods for family and ethnic reasons, a few free souls who simply enjoyed city life—and the poor, who could not afford even the most favorable loan.

The double migration, from city to suburb and rural to city, shook the very foundations of America's cities. Most have been brought to their financial knees.

The meaning of the word *city* changed. Traditionally a city had been a densely populated geographic area which dominated its far less important suburbs. With the postwar migration, the suburbs grew in size, population, wealth, and influence until the word city came to be meaningless except as an archaic political definition. The modern city was transformed into a metropolitan area consisting of the original city and the far-ranging suburbs (sometimes crossing state lines), each politically separate but all bound by common problems. In many instances the old city (now often called the inner city or central core) became smaller than its suburbs, as in Boston, Newark, New Jersey, and Cleveland, Ohio. There are even some very sizeable metropolitan areas that contain no city at all, such as Paterson–Clifton–Passaic, New Jersey, and Anaheim–Santa Ana–Garden Grove, California.*

The central city was buffeted by horrendous problems. Its most

---

* Each of these metropolitan areas, along with San Bernadino-Riverside, California, have over a million residents. But many smaller suburban places have no "downtown." Trumbull, Connecticut, where I reside at this writing, has over 30,000 people and a Main Street, two small and one large shopping centers, but nothing remotely resembling a downtown.

prosperous and self-reliant residents moved to the suburbs. They were followed by the stores that moved into the ubiquitous shopping centers. Many factories, offices, and other places of employment joined the trek to the outskirts. The cities found themselves in a financial squeeze. The exodus of people, stores, and employers lowered the city's tax base and thus its revenues. Those individuals and businesses which remained in the city had to pay higher taxes. This in turn drove still more and more people and employers to the suburbs where taxes were lower.

The suburbs, populated by employed and self-reliant people, needed less community services. In the city, the poor and near poor residents needed far more services—water, sewage, garbage collection, street cleaning, police and fire protection. City schools suffered in quality, both because they lacked funds and because they had to teach more culturally deprived and emotionally scarred youngsters from the ghetto. The suburban communities, needing to offer fewer social services, could lavish funds on education. Some of the nation's great public school systems were built in the affluent green belts around large cities.

That cities must spend more tax money to support poorer residents was demonstrated by a study in New York City in 1972. Computations were made of the city's per capita spending for essential services such as police and fire protection, sanitation, health, education, and human resources in sixty-two city districts. In East Harlem, heavily populated by poor Negroes and Puerto Ricans, the city spent $1,182 a year on each man, woman, and child. A few blocks to the south in the affluent East Side–Yorkville district, the city spent only $278 on each resident. The difference is clearly made up by the ability of the affluent to do private spending for police protection, sanitation, health, and other needed services.

A vicious circle was created in which almost everything that happened in the inner city worsened its problems. High property tax rates shrank the profits of landlords. They had few profits to invest in repairs of the vintage dwellings. There was no incentive to fix up the homes or apartments because repairs would lead to higher property taxes. Besides, there were few in the inner city who could afford to pay higher rents. So, to stay in business, the landlords reduced themselves to slumlords, owning and operating rundown buildings in which every nickel was squeezed out by overcrowding and inadequate maintenance.

Virtually all who could find a way to leave the deteriorating neighborhoods did so, until they were depositories of the trapped, the despairing, and the futile. With precious few exceptions, the businesses that remained in the worst neighborhoods were those making money off poverty, such as those dealing in food, cheap clothing, secondhand furniture, and small loans. Jobs became harder to find and the pay lower. As poverty deepened, the incidence of crime, alcoholism, and drug addiction rose. The poor came to prey upon the poor and the quality of life at times approached a state of surviving in a jungle. More than a few surrendered to despair, apathy, and the tenets of a subculture that knew that only fools hoped for a better life.

Of course, there were many who worked against these trends— individuals working alone or with churches, schools, civil rights, and other organizations. Belatedly, mayors and other political leaders began to realize that the festering sores in the inner cities were dragging down the whole metropolitan area.

Despite inadequate tax resources, mayors and city councils managed to spend rather large sums of money in the inner cities. Police forces were enlarged and more fire protections added. Greater sums were spent on sanitation, health services, education, and recreation. With state and federal financing, some of the worst slums were torn down and replaced with public housing projects. But, as we shall see, these often only worsened the problems.

All of this may be summarized by saying that to one degree or another nearly all of the inner portions of America's great cities were reduced to a hard core of chronically poor people who were largely unable to help themselves and who looked to city governments for aid—aid which most municipalities could not afford.

A DECENT HOME— BUT WHERE?

CHAPTER SIX

Packs of wild dogs run the streets, raiding garbage, attacking people. One of every five homes is without running water and residents go out into the street with buckets. Forty percent of the families are on public welfare. Of the employable people, 30 percent are out of work. There are 20,000 known drug addicts. The more that 130 known youth gangs claim a membership of 9,500. More than 800 violent crimes were committed in the past year.

This is not a description of some teeming area in an emerging nation in a backward portion of the world. It is a part of New York City known as South Bronx.* Poignant (and alarming) accounts of life in South Bronx were provided by reporter Martin Tolchin in *The New York Times* in January, 1973. To go there, he said: ". . . is a journey to a foreign country where fear is the overriding emotion in a landscape of despair."

He also described it as "violent, drugged, burned out, graffiti-splattered and abandoned."

Dr. Harold Wise, founder of the Martin Luther King, Jr., Health Center in the area, said of it: "The South Bronx is a necropolis—a city of death. There's a total breakdown of services, looting is rampant, fires are everywhere."

Tolchin is a good reporter and writer, as the following excerpt indicates:

> *. . . The South Bronx remains home to a twelve-year-old mother of a two-year-old boy, both of whom live with other children in the home of the girl's mother. It is home to women on the streets who appear to be in their mid-forties or fifties, but who are known . . . to be in their early twenties.*
>
> *It is home to a seven-year-old wino, swaying before a build-*

---

* For those unfamiliar with New York City, it is that part of the borough of the Bronx which lies south of the Cross Bronx Expressway. I cannot help but wonder to what extent the building of that elevated highway caused the blighting of the once proud neighborhoods.

ing on the corner of Cypress Avenue and East 138th Street, and to his twelve-year-old addict brother, who injects himself with heroin in a "shooting gallery" in the basement of the building.

It is home to a couple who have finally stopped paying $100 a month for an unheated apartment on Southern Boulevard that has water-soaked walls and mice that run between their two sick children sleeping on floor mattresses. "Why should I pay the landlord to kill me?" the wife asks.

The South Bronx is a community of terrifying extremes.

One health district in the area has an infant mortality rate of 28.3 for every 1,000 live births. The city average is 20.8. New tuberculosis cases average 52.5 for every 1,000 residents, compared with a city average of 32.6 and a national average of twenty-one. The South Bronx had 25 percent of the reported cases of malnutrition in the city last year—2,700 of 10,637. It had about 16 percent of the city's reported cases of venereal disease last year—8,137 of 50,347.

It is a place where the most recent reading scores in some schools indicate that less than 6 percent of the pupils are reading at grade level, a figure that is even worse for all grades than those recorded the previous year.

It is a community where rage always lurks just below the surface and often erupts in acts of seemingly mindless violence. It is a place where a dissenter at a meeting of a Model Cities policy committee was murdered by being dragged into the street and thrown under a moving car. It is where a youngster outside Intermediate School No. 155 on Jackson Avenue in Mott Haven was nearly stomped to death in an argument over a bottle of soda pop.

This litany for South Bronx could go on to great length, but it surely has served its purpose here as an illustration of what author Michael Harrington called *The Other America*. The South Bronx may be a bit worse than slums in other cities of America—or then again it may be only typical. It may safely be said, however, that every non-suburban, industrial city in the land has these problems to some degree.

Nor is the problem of blighted lives distinctive to the cities. Consider the sharecropper grubbing out a few hundred dollars a year through backbreaking work, remaining in debt always to the landlord and the general store. Or, consider the tens of thousands of migrant workers who manage only to sustain a nomadic life by long days of picking fruits and vegetables and worse nights in hovels that are dignified by the name "quarters."

It is the official policy of the United States Government that such housing should not exist. Congress has legislated that every citizen shall occupy "decent" housing. In so doing, the members of Congress probably expressed into law the feelings of every American that in this prosperous land every citizen should enjoy the happiness, security, and comfort of a suitable home.

The desire for a home and the wish for everyone to enjoy it is deeply rooted in the American ethic. The slumlord is an arch villian in this country. If a home is a castle, every person should have one.

And, we have gone to great lengths to make this dream come true. Most Americans are not aware of it, but the housing industry is perhaps the most heavily regulated in the nation. Local, state, and federal governments have been working at the task for at least a century and the result is an almost inconceivable mishmash of laws and regulations.

Perhaps the first purpose of the laws was simply concern for public safety. Many of America's great cities were burned to the ground at one time or another. Among the earliest laws passed were fire regulations, providing for fire escapes, proper furnaces, and use of safe materials in construction.

Epidemics were a menace and in the last century laws were

passed to prevent them—regulations concerning running water, better sanitation facilities, window screens, and much more. Buildings had a way of collapsing, so laws were passed to regulate the quality of construction. Local governments felt the need to have control over the sites where buildings were erected so zoning laws were enacted. New laws were passed almost annually. Administrative departments were created and empowered to impose regulations and codes. The result was a body of rules and statutes on housing that was both immense and bewildering.

The laws and codes led to inspection. It was necessary to make sure the various regulations were being obeyed, so inspectors were sent out to look at fire prevention, health, building construction, elevators, and other aspects of housing. Most of this was highly beneficial. Just try to imagine what it was like to live in American cities back in the days of outdoor privies, stables for horses, unpasteurized milk, and open fires for heating and cooking. We truly do want everyone to have a good home. The nation's dedication to this principle is attested to by the many billions of dollars spent since the 1930's by federal, state, and local governments for public housing.

But the wish confronts some hard realities when a hellhole such as the South Bronx is confronted. Most Americans have heard of slums, as they used to be called, or ghettos, as they are more commonly known today. But few, unless they lived in one, fully realize the despicable life that goes on there. When confronted by articles such as those by reporter Tolchin, there is a tendency to recoil in horror—homes without heat or running water, packs of wild dogs, rampant crime, festering disease. It is something out of the Middle Ages.

As past actions indicate, the majority of Americans are appalled that such squalor exists. They honestly do want to do something about it. But what should be done?

The most appealing, seemingly sensible course of action is to tear down the ghettos and start all over again. Build new, modern apartments and homes that will imbue the occupants with pride and offer them safety and comfort. Erect new schools, design parks and playgrounds, crack down on crime and addiction, beef up sanitation, health, and other services. In short, build whole, new, beautiful communities to replace the ugliness and frustration of the old.

The idea is richly appealing. It fits our American conception of how to solve problems, by building, doing, spending. The old gives way to the new. Technology and engineering will solve our problems.

It is not getting too far ahead of our story to say that the tearing down building anew idea was the grand conception of the 1950's and 1960's. The federal government launched the urban renewal and model cities programs. Their very names, renew and model, reveal their aims. Both have had some outstanding successes. Many downtown areas have been strikingly improved with office buildings, stores, auditoriums, arenas, museums, and parks. Highly attractive apartment complexes have been built for middle and upper income families. And all of this has been good.

But urban renewal and model cities has generally failed to build low-cost housing for lower income families. The reasons for this failure help portray the housing problem in America.

There is no housing fairy godmother to wave her magic wand and instantly create a housing project. The urban renewal project has to be announced and financed, a plan drawn up and approved by various governmental agencies. Then the land has to be purchased and the buildings torn down and the new project erected. All of this takes several years under the best of circumstances. In the meantime, what happened to those ghetto residents who formerly lived there? They were forced to move out to make way for the demolition crews. Generally, they moved into nearby areas. Overcrowding resulted. Competition for the available jobs increased—and so did unemployment. Sometimes with amazing speed, those nearby neighborhoods became slums. Thus, urban renewal, despite the attractive projects that were built, had the effect of worsening the housing problem in inner cities.

There are even greater difficulties involved in tearing down the ghettos and building anew. New dwellings, stores, schools, and parks may have beneficial effects on the quality of life, but they do not attack the causes of what made the place a slum in the first place. New housing and the rest do not make plentiful jobs that alleviate unemployment. Nor do the most attractive of dwellings make the jobs that are available pay enough to raise the wage earner out of poverty. In a word, buildings and parks and the rest do not accomplish very much toward relieving the *causes* of poverty and its resultant frustration, despair, and rage that leads to crime, alcoholism, and addiction.

There are undoubted benefits in terms of better schools, more health clinics, better street lighting, and improved crime control. New apartments and attractive parks undoubtedly are beneficial. But the basic element of poverty remains. And the effects of generations of poverty on life style, personal values, and morality are largely untouched.

Former HUD Secretary Romney calls this a "people crisis" and spoke of it quite frankly in one of his speeches:

> *The city crisis is a people crisis. The population decline is accelerating as fear of crime, neighborhood deterioration, and loss of property value gains strength. A small section of our population has become a real menace to their neighbors. Because we have not been able to get at the social causes of this socially demoralized group—and because we do not know how to protect the much larger group of working poor and dependent poor, as well as moderate income families, from those everyday experiences that generate fear—we are seeing an ac-*

celerated movement to get out of central city areas and out of the central city itself.

Mr. Romney is suggesting, as many others have, that the problems of the ghetto cannot be eliminated until the social ills of a hard core of its residents are alleviated. The severe problems of the South Bronx are not so much houses as people; indeed, the city of New York invested $2.8 million in renovation of housing in the area, only to encounter vandalism and arson. The money was wasted. The Pruitt-Igoe project in St. Louis was built with a prize-winning design, much money, and high hopes. It never was fully occupied and many of those who did move in quickly vacated apartments because of the vandalism and crime in the area. Scores of similar examples could be given.

If rebuilding the slums will not work because the neighborhood morals and morale have deteriorated so badly, it would seem logical, then, to build low-cost housing in more affluent neighborhoods, such as the suburbs. As an intellectual exercise, it makes sense to build dwellings where there are jobs and transportation, hospitals and schools, less violence, an atmosphere of peace, personal responsibility, and striving. Everything would be cheaper and better.

Any such scheme, however, runs into vocal and determined opposition from the residents of the affluent and suburban neighborhoods. The process has been repeated so often in so many cities and towns that a pattern has developed. The project is announced, or perhaps only proposed. The residents quickly unite in their opposition. They form an organization, hold protest rallies, and attend city council or other governmental meetings *en masse*. Various elected officials support them. Court actions are filed to block the project. If the project proceeds as far as the construction stage, there are sometimes open confrontations and violence.

Why the opposition? The prevailing view among white liberals and Negro leaders is that the suburban home owners act out of racial prejudice. A high percentage of the poor and near poor are black or of Spanish-speaking ancestry. They are long-time victims of prejudice in housing and jobs. Indeed, one of the main reasons they are poor and live in ghettos is because of prejudice extending over many generations.

This view of suburban attitudes is certainly supported by long history. Beginning in the 1870's, the nation, North and South, went on a binge of Jim Crow segregation. By law, blacks were segregated on public transportation, in auditoriums and churches, in use of toilets and drinking fountains, on the jobs and at pay windows—and in housing. A skein of devices was developed to herd blacks into ghettos, including laws restricting residency, covenants among home owners, up to violence of the lynching variety.

One of the most effective methods was the infamous "block busting." An unscrupulous realtor would pay a very high price for a house on a block, then sell it to a black family at a loss. Rumors would circulate of other black families moving in. The white residents would be seized with fright. "For Sale" signs would appear overnight on every house, and realtors would gobble them up at a fraction of their former value. Reselling to blacks or cutting them up into rooms or apartments brought a large profit—and all too often, because of the overcrowding, the quick creation of a slum.*

With America's long history of racial segregation, it is difficult to discount it as a cause for suburban opposition to low-cost housing. Yet, there are factors at work other than race. Many of the poor and near poor, who might conceivably occupy low-cost housing, are white. Their numbers include the elderly, the young

---

* Many of the white neighborhoods turned black and lost nothing in attractiveness or real estate values. To belabor the obvious, there is nothing about race, religion, ethnic background, or sex that creates a slum. Also, some neighborhoods resisted block busting by welcoming the black families into the area.

whose earning power is low, and significant numbers of whites of any age whose income is low for whatever reason.* A number of studies have shown that the violent, desperate life-style in a place such as the South Bronx is not a product of race, but of poverty. The very poor of any race or ethnic background tend to develop similar problems.

Further evidence that racial prejudice may not be the only reason for suburban opposition to low-cost housing is the relatively painless movement of significant numbers of middle and upper income blacks to the suburbs or to safer, more affluent city neighborhoods. The millenium of brotherly love has not yet arrived, but in recent years an increasing number of more well-to-do black families have integrated formerly lily-white neighborhoods and towns without causing panic. It is a rare suburb which does not have at least a few black families.

Some social observers have begun to suggest fairly recently that suburbanites engage in prejudice all right, but against the poor more than the black. The poor of whatever age, skin color, or religious persuasion are viewed as a whole series of threats. The poor may take jobs by working for less wages. Their presence may lower real estate values. This is a serious threat because, if you will remember from Chapter Two, the whole system of financing and construction is built on the assumption that the housing market will rise (or at least not decline).

The suburbanite also fears that the poor will bring their culture with them. Local school standards will be lowered; violence, crime, and drug addiction of the ghetto may follow the poor to the suburbs. At the very least, taxes will rise because the poor will create increased need for police, health, and welfare services.

That suburban prejudice is more against poverty than race is in-

* The Federation of Jewish Philanthropies in New York City reported in 1973 that there were 140,000 Jewish families in the metropolis with incomes of under $6,000 a year.

dicated by some other evidence. This may be illustrated in a single town located on the fringes of a middle-sized East Coast city that has a large poor population. The suburban town has a population of over 30,000. Residents are middle class. Most are either skilled blue collar workers or lower echelon white collar workers. The poor are kept out by reducing employment opportunities almost to nil. There is virtually no industry of any variety. There is one large shopping center and it is located on the border of the neighboring city. The other stores consist of food, drug, and other convenience stores. There are only a handful of gas stations. Only two restaurants may be found.

The town covers a large area, so it is nearly impossible to get around other than by car. There are no sidewalks in case anyone wanted to walk in safety. The town is linked to the city by one bus trip a day, fare for which is fifty cents one way.

All of this is done with considerable calculation. Early in 1973, application was made to the town hall for a zoning change to permit erection of a small convalescent home for elderly people. Petitions were immediately circulated to block it. Asked what was wrong with a convalescent home in the town, the petition passer replied, "Nothing, but you never know where it will lead. A convalescent home this week, something else next. Soon the town will be ruined."

In his view, the price of keeping out the poor is eternal vigilance.

Whatever the reason, be it prejudice against blacks or the poor or both, suburban communities do not want low-cost housing and fight it with every possible resource.

An instant problem is created. Americans may believe that every family ought to have a decent home. But where? Low-cost housing doesn't seem to work in the ghetto and the suburbs don't want it. The poor, working or otherwise, are thus passed into an American limbo. According to the dictionary, limbo is "a place or condition of neglect or oblivion to which unwanted things or persons are relegated.'' The word also has a theological meaning in the Christian religion; Limbo is the region bordering on Hell.

We have drawn with some pains a picture of the housing problem in the United States. To review briefly, any housing in the United States is very expensive and getting more so. Middle class and even well-to-do families spend a large portion of their income on shelter, perhaps as much as one-half. The cost of home ownership makes it very difficult for lower income families to acquire property and all but impossible for the near poor and poor, who are instead relegated to blighted neighborhoods where the quality of life deteriorates sharply.

As discouraging as the problem may seem, there are solutions. Many have been tried and most of them have a record of partial, sometimes total failure. These failures have lent an aura of discouragement to all efforts to solve the low-cost housing problem.

In the next section of the book, we will consider those solutions that have been tried and why they have failed. Following that, we will consider some other ideas, not yet widely tried, which seem to offer some hope for the future.

SOLUTIONS

PART TWO

PUBLIC HOUSING: COMBATING UGLINESS AND CRIME

CHAPTER SEVEN

Is the public housing program of the United States a $100 billion failure worthy only of being scrapped, as Secretary Romney and many others contend? Or, have its considerable virtues been lost sight of in the vast publicity over its mistakes? Has public housing been made a whipping boy for a lot of social and governmental ills only distantly related to housing?

These are important questions in the 1970's. A tide of conservative thinking seems to be sweeping the nation. Even liberals are engaging in soul searching over the "failure of liberalism." It is alleged that governmental agencies have improperly administered the high-minded social programs adopted over the last forty years. Public housing is cited as among the foremost fiascos.

Conservatives point to the failures in the housing programs (along with those in education, public health, welfare, and other social programs) as proof of the integral bankruptcy of the liberal belief that government must assist people to do what they cannot accomplish themselves. Programs such as public housing are derided as "permissive." Conservatives call for a return to the work ethic and self-reliance. In his second inaugural address, President Nixon sounded this theme in these words:

> *A person can be expected to act responsibly only if he has responsibility. This is human nature. So let us encourage individuals at home and nations abroad to do more for themselves and decide more for themselves. Let us locate more responsibility in more places. Let us measure what we will do for others by what they will do for themselves.*
>
> *That is why I offer no promise of a purely governmental solution for every problem. We have lived too long with that false promise. In trusting too much to government, we have asked of it more than it can deliver. This leads only to inflated expectations, to reduced individual effort, and to a disappointment and frustration that erode confidence both in what government can*

> *do and in what people can do.*
>
> *Government must learn to take less from people so people can do more for themselves.*
>
> *Let each of us remember that America was built not by government, but by people; not by welfare, but by work; not by shirking responsibility but by seeking responsibility.*
>
> *In our own lives, let each of us ask not just what will government do for me, but what can I do for myself?*

President Nixon did more than just talk about such a course of action. By impounding funds previously appropriated by Congress, he indicated a cutback in federal spending for social programs. In January, 1973, he imposed a freeze on all new federal housing programs.

This action was applauded by many people: with the possible exception of the public welfare system, no federal program has drawn more wrath than public housing. Critics have carped at it since its inception in 1937. And, in fact, there has been no shortage of mistakes and abuses to criticize. There are few matters in America more controversial than public housing programs.

Let us nonetheless try to wend our way through the controversy in search of how the public housing system operates and make some judgments of its virtues and faults. In so doing, perhaps we can arrive at some evaluation of the larger question: the role of government in solving social problems.

The federal government entered the field of public housing with the National Housing Act of 1937. That basic law has been amended many times by various Congresses. New laws and programs have been added. There has been so much legislative tinkering with housing legislation since 1937 that a legal labyrinth has been created. The complexity of the laws is perhaps the very first problem. In an article in the February, 1972, issue of *Fortune* magazine entitled "Housing Subsidies are a Grand Delusion," writer Gurney Breckenfeld made this comment:

> *The (housing) subsidy machinery has grown so intricate that it confuses even housing experts. A whole profession of consultants has arisen to help baffled mayors, legislators, and project sponsors find their way through the regulatory thickets. George Romney . . . for two years has pleaded unsuccessfully with Congress to simplify the tangle. Not long ago he complained to a House subcommittee that "These housing-subsidy programs are so complicated that they are practically impossible of administration.**

There are at least twenty-two separate programs for providing federal subsidies to renters, home owners, and financial institutions.

We begin to understand the federal housing programs when we realize that the term "public housing" is a misnomer, a sort of catch-all phrase for programs that have relatively little to do with housing the poor. Many of those carping at "public housing" probably do not have in mind the highly successful FHA system for insuring home mortgages. Few critics are suggesting doing away with FHA insurance.

What most people have in mind when they speak of public housing are the high-rise apartment buildings built and operated by "the government" in inner cities for housing the poor. The buildings, at least in the public view, are uniformly dreary. All seem to be made of brick and look alike, reddish-brown eyesores standing stilletto-like amid barren, often blacktopped open spaces.

There are such structures, plenty of them, and great publicity has attended them as schools of crime and hotbeds of violence where the "shiftless" and "ne'er-do-well" live off the tax dollars

---

* Similar criticisms have been made about nearly every other federal program. The need for fewer, more simplified, easily understood and administered programs is apparently chronic in the federal government. The present maze of programs leads not only to wasteful duplication, but sometimes to programs that work at cross purposes and are mutually-defeating.

of wage earners. Some of these public housing projects, such as the famous Pruitt-Igoe in St. Louis, have had so much vandalism, so many muggings and rapes that the decent people have moved out, leaving the structures either inhabited by the most criminal elements of the population or abandoned entirely.

These are facts. They are true. But to suggest that all public housing projects are like this or that this is all that happens in public housing is to make an absurd exaggeration. It is akin to saying that because there are plane crashes all planes are unsafe or that because there are shoplifters all shoppers are thieves.

Viewed objectively, there is much about public housing to recommend. There are immense obstacles and some bad mistakes have been made, yet public housing may be one of the very best programs operated by the federal government. It is difficult to understand why so many conservatives have attacked it, for it operates in a manner which many conservatives urge as a remedy for the ills of the federal bureaucracy.

In an article entitled "Public Housing—Success or Failure?" in the *George Washington Law Review,* housing official George R. Genung, Jr., termed public housing "unique" among government programs. It subsists on federal subsidies, yet it is or was intended to be locally administered and locally controlled. Moreover, until very recently it was one of the few, financially self-supporting government programs.

As originally designed, a Local Housing Authority (LHA) is created in a city, town, or county to build and operate low-cost housing for the indigent. The local authority applies to the Department of Housing and Urban Development for permission to build a given number of units of such housing. Upon receiving permission, the LHA borrows money to develop and construct the housing units. The loan is repaid in the form of a forty-year, tax exempt, local housing authority bonds. These are sold much in the manner of any other local bonds issued to build schools, highways, or public buildings. The major difference is that the federal government guarantees to pay the principle and interest on the bonds.

The LHA is expected to operate and maintain the buildings from rents received from tenants. Because the federal government assumes the major charges of debt service, it was expected that rents could be set at low enough figures to really benefit the poor.

That is essentially what happened. Local authorities built projects, charged low rents, yet were financially successful—at least for many years. In recent years the success has come unstuck through a variety of circumstances.

There are nearly 3,000 local housing authorities in the United States providing housing for more than three million low income families. The authorities range in size from that in New York City, which operates 150,000 units, to one in Alabama operating only four units. Contrary to the public image of those high-rise, red brick jungles, most housing projects are small. Only 173 authorities, less than 6 percent of the total, operate more than 1,000 units. Only another 114 authorities or less than 4 percent manage from 500 to 1,000 units. Thus, no more than one in ten authorities operate what can be considered large projects.

Nor is ugliness any longer a characteristic of public housing. Most smaller projects consist of highly attractive clusters of distinctive one and two story townhouses or garden apartments surrounded by lawns and trees and playgrounds. Red brick has given way to stone and wood, large windows and shutters. Many of the small projects are, if anything, indistinguishable from privately built condominiums. The uninformed passerby would not recognize them as public housing projects.

The high-rise, high density apartment buildings have also left the red brick jungles far behind. Nearly all are made of modern curtain wall or poured concrete. Apartments are open to fresh air with private balconies to enjoy the view. The buildings are not noticeably different from newly-built private apartments and hotels.

Americans are simply less aware of these new styles in public housing projects, perhaps because the projects themselves are less noticeable. They enhance, rather than detract from, their neighborhoods. Yet, the image of the brick eyesores lingers on—probably because those buildings linger on.

The older buildings are more than a public relations problem. They are monuments to mistakes of the past. Many were built as cheaply as possible as sort of "halfway houses" where the poor could stop briefly on their way to prosperity. Such accoutrements as interior doors, adequate light fixtures, even toilet seats were left out in the name of economy. Not uncommonly, elevators did not stop at every floor. Some of these buildings have been mercifully demolished, but many remain. A few have undergone expensive remodeling with modern kitchens and bathrooms. Walls have been knocked out to re-shape and enlarge apartments. More open space, planted with trees and shrubs, has been provided. All this is progress, but a great deal more needs to be done to correct past errors. Mr. Genung commented on this:

> *The temporary housing of yesterday has become the older, permanent housing of today. If public housing officials knew then what we know now, it is quite possible that things would have been done differently. It seems both unfair and unproductive to belittle their efforts because the "rules of the game" have changed. Rather, we must deal with the present, measuring the new public housing we are building today against our present standards, and deciding whether the program is succeeding. There is no question that it is.*

The older, high-rise buildings are an immense problem to housing authorities. They are expensive to maintain, if for no other reason than simple age. The cost of maintenance eats into LHA operating funds. Erstwhile financially successful projects are now on the verge of bankruptcy, in part because of high maintenance costs.

The older high-rise buildings are also centers of crime— vandalism, murder, arson, rape, and robbery. Studies have shown that crime increases sharply with the height of the building in public housing projects. To live on the upper floors is to be in peril.

These findings contrast sharply with crime figures in high-rise apartment buildings for middle and upper income families. There the crime rate lowers as buildings rise.

The crime and violence in urban public housing projects has provided fuel for critics who would abandon the whole idea of housing the poor. The rationale goes something like this: These housing projects have been built at the taxpayers' expense. The apartments are surely much better than the tenants had in the slums. Yet, they don't appreciate it. The buildings are vandalized. The tenants prey on each other. They don't appreciate what has been done for them: "You can take the person out of the slum, but you can't take the slum out of the person." The government ought to forget the whole business and save the taxpayers' money. The poor should go to work and save their money and get ahead just like everyone else did.

Perhaps. But there are other ways of looking at the crime problem in public housing projects, ways that do not call for abandoning the whole concept of public housing. For starters, some of the projects with high crime rates merely reflect the deteriorating neighborhoods in which they are located. Criminals from nearby streets enter the projects to attack the tenants.

Efforts are being made to reduce such invasions. The New York Housing Authority spends $10 million a year on security and has the fourth largest police force in the nation after the cities of New York, Chicago, and Los Angeles. Its effectiveness is being undermined because the regular New York Police Department has reduced its activities in housing projects because of the presence of the housing authority police. The net effect has not been more police protection for tenants, but a form of subsidy to the city which is supposed to police the projects. There is also more than a little jealousy and friction between the two types of policemen. The Chicago Housing Authority is using a variety of methods, including television monitoring of buildings. Search is on for still other ways to improve security in projects.

More provocative analysis of the crime problem comes from Oscar Newman, author of the book *Defensible Space*. He studied a number of high crime projects (including Pruitt-Igoe) as well as others where crime was low, seeking explanations for the violence. In an interview in *Time* magazine in November, 1972, he described some of his findings:

> *The idea of defensible space first emerged back in 1964, when I was part of a team of architects and sociologists who were studying why the notorious Pruitt-Igoe public housing project in St. Louis was being torn apart by the people who live in it. Every public area—the lobbies, the laundries and mail rooms—were a mess, literally. There was human excrement in the halls. Except in one small area on each floor of each building. You had to go through a fire door and then you were in a little hallway separating two apartments. This little hall was spotless—you could eat off the floor. When we called out to each other in the other hallways, we could hear people bolting and chaining their doors, but in this area we heard peepholes click open. Sometimes people even opened their doors. The reason was that they felt this little hallway was an extension of their own apartments. We knew then we were on to something.*

Mr. Newman concluded that one of the reasons higher buildings have more crime is that they are more anonymous. Tenants do not identify them as their homes. Moreover, the buildings are full of angled corridors and blind public areas where the majority of crimes are committed. The staircases required by fire regulations provide criminals with alternate means of escape.

Mr. Newman indicated that architects have erred in designing public projects to offer tenants privacy. Typically, buildings open on to inner courtyards and playgrounds. This privacy shelters intruders and criminals. Newman believes the buildings should open on to the streets where there is automobile traffic, and pedestrians and where intruders are visible. Privacy is possible for middle and upper income apartment dwellers who are able to hire doormen and guards, but is not wise in low income projects.

Providing the tenants with a sense of territory will also reduce the crime rate, Mr. Newman believes. No more than six apartments should open on to a common hallway. Beyond that number, tenants tend to look upon it as a public place, rather than their private dwelling. This feeling of personal occupancy can be enhanced by fences, play equipment, benches, better lighting, name plates, and the like. With this feeling of personal occupancy, as against public anonymity, comes pride and a desire to defend the residence against both intruders and fellow tenants who damage the quality of life.

Mr. Newman's ideas have been adopted as guidelines by HUD, the New York State Urban Development Corporation, and city housing authorities in Chicago, Philadelphia, and Minneapolis. He is currently working on a $2 million grant from HUD to modify four existing projects in New York City to carry out his principles.

The crime problem in older projects is serious, but using it as a reason to abandon public housing is a case of throwing the baby out with the bathwater.

OTHER PROBLEMS IN PUBLIC HOUSING

CHAPTER EIGHT

In 1968, the late President Lyndon B. Johnson shocked the nation and the housing industry by asking that over 100,000 units of public housing a year be built until every American had a decent home. He envisioned the construction of 1,226,000 new units in ten years, a figure which Congress adopted.

The reaction of shock stemmed from the fact that no one, including public housing officials, thought it was possible. One hundred thousand units a year was more than three times the number built in 1967 and five times the number erected in prior years. Indeed, it was axiomatic in the industry that no more than 35,000 units could be built in a single year. To suggest 100,000 units seemed visionary.

This belief was destroyed in the flurry of building activity. Housing authorities began to use a new technique, the so-called "turnkey" construction. These are projects built by private developers and sold to housing authorities. This method is believed to be cheaper and faster than construction performed by the Local Housing Authorities.

Public housing authorities proved not only that they could build 100,000 units a year, but that they could have built and managed twice that number had funds been made available to them. George R. Genung, Jr., goes even further:

> *There is no doubt that the local housing authorities today could produce a half-million housing units a year. At that level, the country could proceed to eliminate the problem of substandard housing for persons with low incomes. It would also be possible for these authorities to provide middle-income housing. To bring about these changes would require a commitment to change—by the Congress, the President, the mayors and city councils, and especially the Local Housing Authorities.*

What changes? Clearly a greater commitment on the part of taxpayers will be needed. The high construction costs that have driven up the price of private homes also affect public housing. During 1971 and 1972 public housing construction stayed at about the 100,000 level, despite a backlog of demand for four times that number, simply because rising costs absorbed the limited appropriations.

The Nixon administration has shown considerable ambivalence toward public housing. In 1970, 1971, and part of 1972, it seemed to favor public housing as a means of stimulating the economy and ending the economic recession.

Yet, as his second inaugural address indicated, Mr. Nixon has a philosophical dislike for federally sponsored social programs. He believes in self-help rather than government "handouts." With the upturn in the economy in 1972, Mr. Nixon refused to spend the many millions of dollars which Congress had appropriated for public housing. He maintained that such spending would be inflationary, that is, it would lead to an enlarged money supply and higher prices.

There are many who approve of Mr. Nixon's attitude toward housing. They feel the programs are a failure and lead to permissive laziness among the poor. Others lament the President's actions, among them Mr. Genung:

> *The unfortunate aspect of the retardation of any program is that the momentum which has been generated can be lost. The nation as a whole, as well as the poor, will be the loser if this occurs. The Kerner Commission [on the causes of violence] was explicit in describing the feelings and reactions of the poor who sense that the country really does not care. The country can scarcely afford to turn its back on the housing needs of this segment of the population. It would be foolhardy and dangerous to return production to the inadequate level of a few years ago. Local Housing Authorities, having learned from past experience, are proving that they can do the job and do it well. They should be given every opportunity to continue this momentum.*

Perhaps. But there is already considerable evidence of financial strain among many of the Local Housing Authorities. The larger ones, in particular, have been losing money for some years, despite stringent economies in staff, maintenance, and other activities. In 1972, the Chicago Housing Authority expected to lose $5 million on its operations. At least forty Authorities expected to have exhausted all their financial reserves by the middle of 1973 and be unable to pay their bills. It seemed likely that at least some would go bankrupt.

The basic cause of the financial distress is that the fiscal arrangements for operating the housing authorities, which were highly successful in the 1940's, had broken down by the 1970's. Rents paid by tenants were to offset the operating costs of the housing projects and to provide for reserve funds to be used in some future "rainy day" which the Authorities might encounter. Any additional funds collected by the LHA's were to be returned to the federal government to help defray the costs of the debt service. This was an excellent arrangement in the 1940's and 1950's. Housing Authorities were so well off that Congress reduced the amount Authorities were permitted to place into reserves so that the amount of the federal contribution could be decreased.

By the 1970's, yesterday's financial success had turned into a financial quagmire. And little of the blame could be placed on the Local Housing Authorities.

The same price inflation which has belabored Americans in all walks of life has plagued the LHA's. Everything involved in operating and maintaining the housing went up in price, and older buildings required more repairs and renovation. A particular squeeze resulted when municipal employees, including those in housing projects, organized and demanded higher salaries and wages. In a word, costs went *up*—and then increased.

There was nothing in the rental arrangement, however, to permit the income of housing authorities to keep pace. Rents were pegged on a variety of complicated formulae based upon the income of the tenants. Those who earned more paid more. But in general 21.9 percent of the net family income of tenants was paid as rent.

As operating costs rose, housing authorities raised rents. But there was danger that such increases would be self-defeating, that is, the rents would become so high that the poor could not afford to live in public housing. In this context, it should be remembered that the incomes of the poor did not keep pace with the inflated prices. The working poor, as well as those living on public welfare or social security, were caught in a squeeze of relatively stable incomes and ever rising prices for the essentials of life.

In 1969, the Brooke Amendment (introduced by Senator Edward W. Brooke of Massachusetts) was passed. It prohibited public housing authorities from charging more than 25 percent of tenant income for rent. Congress appropriated $75 million to reimburse housing authorities for any operating losses.

The funds were immediately tied up by HUD, whose officials argued with Congress and local housing authorities over how the law should be carried out. Congress restated its intent in the 1970 housing act and raised the appropriated funds to $150 million. By 1973 not one penny of this money had been made available to LHA's. The financial crisis and threat of bankruptcy was the result.

Critics of the Nixon administration see this action as proof of the administration's less than enthusiastic support of housing programs and their distrust of housing authorities. Whether or not that is true, a more cogent reason for the holdup in funds has been offered by Norman V. Watson, assistant HUD secretary for housing management:

> *We are now completing a new subsidy formula that will offset the effects of the Brooke Amendment. Nobody is suggesting that the federal government will stop providing subsidy money. But*

we are setting a ceiling. The local authorities will have to be more responsible and efficient. The old practice of spending whatever they think they need and then coming to the federal government for reimbursement is going to end.

A new formula has been widely advocated. The 1937 formula just doesn't seem to work in 1973. The process by which Congress appropriates extra funds to "bail out" housing authorities that are losing money seems at best a stopgap measure. Many observers have pointed to the need for a new method of financing public housing projects to return them to their former basis of fiscal solvency. The Nixon administration seems to be promising this.

There are other problems facing housing authorities which must be solved if the long time American dream of slum eradication is to be achieved. A major one is site selection. As we saw earlier, everyone is for housing the poor—as long as they are housed in somebody else's backyard.

Under Mr. Romney, HUD promoted the "fair share" plan, a somewhat patronizing variation on the old Colonial concept of the "white man's burden." The idea was that suburban communities would take their fair share of public housing units. If everyone accepted a few poor people into their midst, no one community would be burdened with a deluge of them. The idea received considerable acceptance and a good bit of site dispersal of housing units occurred. Some indigent families liked the system, for it gave them an opportunity to move out of ghettos into more secure neighborhoods with better schools and environment.

Opposition came, however, from community leaders, principally black. One of the effects of site dispersal, as they saw it, was to dilute the bloc voting strength of blacks and other minority groups. Only in recent years had blacks learned to vote as a bloc to elect councilmen, mayors, members of Congress, and other officials. These black officeholders were beginning to use the political process to make gains for the minority group.

Also, site dispersal put housing authorities squarely in the middle of the integration-segregation controversy. Until the mid-1960's, integration was the nearly universal goal of black leaders. Men such as Dr. Martin Luther King, Jr., wanted the black man to have equal rights and equal opportunities so he could be amalgamated into the nation as any other citizen. Many, perhaps most, blacks still see this as the goal. But a new idea is advocated by other, often younger, black leaders. They see segregation as a virtue. By remaining ghettoized, black people can enhance their culture and customs and thus their pride. They can develop political and economic strength apart from white people. They fear black culture will be diluted and lost in overwhelmingly white America. When Negroes are divided over the integration-segregation issue, housing officials find it difficult to chart a safe course through the controversy.

Some students of the public housing problem believe that site selection could be eased if public housing authorities were made full-fledged taxpayers. Under existing arrangements, public housing projects are exempt from local property taxes, the chief source of municipal revenues. But the LHA's pay 10 percent of their net rents received in lieu of taxes. For this amount the city government is to provide all its accustomed services, such as police and fire protection, garbage collection, street cleaning, education, health and welfare services. In the early years of public housing, the arrangement seemed fair. More recently, with property taxes on the rise, municipalities feeling the financial pinch, and the poor needing greater city services, the arrangement is anything but profitable for city governments.

If housing projects were fully self-supporting and tax paying, several benefits would result. Public housing would suddenly become more attractive to city governments and to citizens. Instead of being burdens to local taxpayers, public housing projects would have become assets—moneymakers. Many site selection problems would disappear. Housing authorities would suddenly find more and better land available. There would be less need to cram many units into hard-to-police, high-rise structures on marginal, unattractive sites. Projects should spread out more, with low-rise buildings and more open space. They could be located nearer to existing school, shopping, and other community facilities. Also, city officials would feel encouraged to provide a higher level of city services to taxpaying citizens residing in public projects.

Site selection could also be improved were local housing authorities granted greater independence in determining where projects are to be built. As it now stands, housing authorities are quasi-independent branches of the local government. There can be no public housing program unless local governing officials approve the application for federal funds. Often the power to veto a project is the power to control it. Thus, housing officials feel behooved to seek municipal approval for a site, even if it is not strictly necessary. In some jurisdictions it is required. In six states, including California, voter approval is needed through a referendum before a site is approved.

Such procedures leave site selection vulnerable to all the passions of the moment and to political expedience. Marginal sites that are offensive to the fewest people are often chosen—in the midst of a bad neighborhood in the ghetto, for example. Public housing in the United States would clearly improve if housing authorities were granted greater power to choose the best, most feasible site. The courts or some other responsible body could be empowered to review the selected site to guard against untoward abuses by housing officials.

One final problem of public housing needs discussion here— tenant control. This is a fairly recent issue. It was not even considered back in the days when occupancy of public housing was viewed as a temporary state on the way to affluence. But today, public housing is long term and even permanent quarters for many people. Many tenants are demanding the right to participate in the management of the project. Tenants want better crime control, maintenance, and social services. They believe that project managers are unresponsive to these needs.

The most frequently heard charge is that housing officials are white and from middle class backgrounds, while the tenants are poor and black. The tenants contend that the managers do not understand them and their problems.

In his previously cited article, Mr. Genung suggested that while tenants ought to bark they may be barking up the wrong tree. Local officials receive the complaints because they are the most visible and accessible to tenants, but in Mr. Genung's view many of the problems lie in Washington and out of the control of local officials.

A Local Housing Authority official cannot be totally responsive to all of the factions that are either involved or interested in the public housing program. In our democratic society, a public body, such as a housing authority board, often finds itself trying to serve many "masters." The local authority must be responsive to HUD, which pays a major portion of the program costs. Within that federal agency structure, there are many divergent points of view, each having some effect on the local authority's decision process. The demands of the social service-oriented branch of HUD are often in complete contradiction to those of the fiscal management branch. For example, although HUD is continually requesting local authorities to provide increased tenant services, it will not permit the local agency to spend the money needed to implement service programs. After many years of laboring under this ambivalence, local housing officials tend to turn a deaf ear toward reforms until shown that they have the capacity to pay for them. Critics then tend to write off public housing officials as being unresponsive.

Mr. Genung cited as another example the compromises housing officials must make with politicians and citizen groups on site selection. He concluded:

> *It is most difficult for them (tenants) to understand and accept the conflicting pressures that affect the decision-making process at the local authority. Good communication between management and tenants is, therefore, more essential than ever before. Unless this communication improves, bringing about mutual understanding, the public housing program may become the very thing its critics claim it is.*

Clearly, if this view is correct, tenants might be more effective if they joined with local officials to try to bring pressure on Washington to change its policies and regulations. The exact opposite, however, is often the case. An example occurred late in 1972 in Philadelphia, where the Resident Advisory Board, created in 1969, was said to represent 120,000 tenants in forty-two public housing projects.

A confrontation soon developed between the board and city officials. Mayor Frank L. Rizzo, newly elected as a hard-line conservative, ousted the housing director and appointed a temporary director, Gilbert Stein, with orders to clean out "old cheaters" and undesirables among tenants. The Resident Advisory Board and Mr. Stein clashed. The board claimed that Rizzo and Stein were seeking "to decimate the political strength of Northern black urbanites." Stein replied that the board did not really represent the tenants and ordered an election among tenants to determine if the Advisory Board should continue to represent them. The outcome of the vote truly didn't matter, for a political issue had been formed over what was a purely practical matter of operating the best possible housing projects. Philadelphia had long been considered to have one of the best housing authorities in the nation. The political confrontation could only lessen its effectiveness.

The Philadelphia situation also illustrates another common problem in public housing. It is not intended as a criticism of Mayor Rizzo to point out that he was fostering public fears in his campaign to weed out cheaters and criminals from the public housing projects. Fraud does exist.* It is rather simple to accomplish. A variety of incomes may be hidden and not declared. If the full income were reported, the tenant would have to pay a higher rent or be ineligible for public housing at all. This might be lamented in that such "wealthy" and cheating tenants may keep legitimately deserving poor from finding the public housing which they desperately need. It is certain that at least some of this extra income comes from illegal sources, welfare fraud, or rackets. Likewise it is certain that some of these people prey on other tenants in projects and that no one would like them ousted more than their own neighbors.

In any event, headline-grabbing campaigns to crack down on cheaters does more harm than good. Cheaters should be weeded out, to be sure, but it could be done quietly and with less political noise. At best a small percentage of tenants will be removed, but

---

* About 1960, when I was a newspaperman, I wrote a prolonged exposé of welfare fraud in the city of Baltimore. My newspaper ran the articles describing how the fraud occurred. The Department of Welfare was encouraged to crack down on defrauders and it did so. Then, the campaign insisted that the State's Attorney bring the culprits to trial. This was done and convictions occurred. In all honesty, it is not an episode which I view with much pride today. I failed to understand then, as I now do, that the welfare system encouraged fraud—and the system has not improved an iota to this day. I was, I believe, hounding a lot of poor people who had little chance to live in decency other than by breaking a rather foolish law. The law provided that welfare be paid only when there was no man living in the home. Many couples cheated by having the wife claim she had been abandoned, when in fact the man lived at home at least some of the time. The problem was the law, which forced the breakup of families, and not the poor who sought ways to take advantage of it. I believe something similar may be said about housing fraud. When one is very poor and struggling, moral and legal niceties have a tendency to take a back seat to expediency.

the headlines suggest a much larger number and undermine understanding of public housing and the need for it.

In this and the previous chapter I have tried to describe public housing and its problems. What may be concluded from all this?

It seems to me—and others may disagree on the basis of the same facts—that the public and political hysteria over public housing projects is unjustified. In the main, public housing seems to work rather well. There are exceptions, such as Pruitt-Igoe. There are problems, such as excessive regulation at the federal level, site selection, tenant participation, underfinancing, and others which have been mentioned. Mistakes have been made in site selection, architecture, and management. There is a certain amount of fraud. These are serious matters, but some corrections have already occurred. Human ingenuity and determination certainly ought to be able to make many further improvements. A new financing formula is certainly in order.

But, in balance, it seems to me that the positive aspects of public housing projects far outweigh the negative. The system of decentralized local control of the projects may well be ideal in a nation such as ours; the breakdown may have come from failure to use this system sufficiently well, imposing too many controls from Washington. The system has permitted a great deal of public housing to be built. It has been adaptable over a thirty-five-year period to new goals, increased needs, new technology, altered family desires, and improved styles in architecture.

It seems to me, further, that these projects still offer, perhaps more than ever, the fulfillment of the goals first set in the 1930's—eradication of slums and construction of decent housing for all Americans. No other tested method is in sight by which so much housing can be built so fast for the poorest of our citizens.

What is needed is more emphasis on the positive. It is passing strange how much has been written about Pruitt-Igoe and other high crime projects and how little about the vast quantities of attractive new housing that has been built more recently. It is equally strange how much emphasis is placed on a relative handful of cheaters and how little on the many working poor, elderly, widowed, and orphaned who benefit so greatly from public housing. Strangest of all is the emphasis that suggests that the tenants of public housing are somehow shiftless spongers at the public trough. Emphasizing the positive, it seems to me, would explain to middle and upper income taxpayers the great economic and social benefits *they* receive when the poor are better housed, fed, and clothed.

But, in truth, most of the talk of the failure of public housing is not really directed at the local public housing projects. The abuses and sense of failure are involved in two unfortunate federal housing programs known as Section 235 and 236. It is these we take up next.

THE SCANDAL OF SUBSIDIZED HOUSING

CHAPTER NINE

The United States government has perhaps made few blunders of greater magnitude than its 1968 venture into subsidized housing.* This is the $100 billion mistake Secretary Romney referred to. Others have estimated the eventual cost at twice that amount. Most tragically, subsidized housing only worsened the ills it sought to correct.

In the mid-1960's, the nation was rocked by a series of violent riots in the ghettos of more than 100 cities, notably Los Angeles, Newark, Detroit, Chicago, Washington, and Cleveland. Police, national guardsmen, and even federal troops had difficulty quelling the fighting, shooting, looting, and burning. Many lives were lost; property damage ran into the billions of dollars; tens of thousands were made homeless and jobless.

Repeated analyses of the causes of the riots led to the conclusion that they were a spontaneous expression of the pent-up frustration and fury of ghetto residents, mostly black, at their second class status, lack of civil rights, economic discrimination, joblessness, inferior education, and substandard housing.

Lyndon Johnson was in the White House. Perhaps more than any other president he had empathy for the poor and downtrodden in America. Born in humble circumstances himself, he sought to help the indigent, black, Mexican-American, Puerto Rican, Indian, orphaned, elderly, uneducated, and sick. In 1964, he was elected president by the largest margin in American history.** Quickly, he launched a program of progressive legislation almost

---

* I am joining other writers in using the term subsidized housing to distinguish it from public housing projects, which were discussed in the last two chapters. Public housing has many assets, as we saw. Subsidized housing under Sections 235 and 236 (added to the National Housing Act in 1968) has few defenders. Unfortunately, the distinction is not always made by writers and commentators, leading an understandably confused public to assume that all housing programs are a failure and a waste.

** President Johnson received over 61 percent of the vote; in 1972 President Nixon got slightly under that although he carried forty-nine states.

unprecedented in America—civil rights and voting rights legislation, Medicare for the elderly, aid to education, model cities, antipollution laws, consumer protection acts, and much more.

Among his programs was a vast increase in new public housing. He called for 100,000 units of public housing a year. He also suggested two other programs, which Congress adopted, that were hoped would provide a "decent" home for every American and go far toward relieving the causes of the disastrous riots, greatly accelerate the nation's construction of low-cost housing, and quickly eliminate slums—subsidized housing.

On paper it was a good idea, one advocated for many years by economists, sociologists, and experts in the field of housing. In fact many people who lament the failures of the 235 and 236 Programs, as they are called, still believe the basic idea is the only one that will ever work to solve the housing problem.

The 235 and 236 Programs seek to bring the ingenuity and energy of the private housing industry and individual home buyers into the search for low-cost housing. Private builders had long avoided low-cost housing, because there was very little money in it compared to the handsome profits from middle and upper income construction. With 235 and 236, the federal government sought to change this by offering builders a subsidy for erecting low-cost housing, much as the government pays subsidies to farmers, shipbuilders, airlines, and a host of other industries which Congress feels need to be encouraged because they are valuable to the people or the nation.

The law enacted by Congress also subsidized home ownership by enabling the poor and near poor to purchase new or older homes (or to rent apartments), fix them up, and maintain them. It was felt the American desire for a home of a family's own would go a long way toward eradicating the slums.

Section 235 (applying to homes) and Section 236 (applying to apartments) of the housing act were the mechanisms for providing the subsidies. On paper it is rather simple. Section 235 helps low income families buy new or older homes. The Federal Housing Administration insures the mortgage and subsidizes part of the monthly payments. There are various complicated formulae, based on the size and income of the family, for figuring how much subsidy the family receives from the government. In general, it may be said that families of four people with incomes of $7,000 to $8,000 a year were able to buy modest homes for about $200 down. Their mortgage could not exceed $21,000. The buyers were expected to spend at least 20 percent of their income for mortgage payments, while the federal government paid the rest. Incomes are periodically examined, and subsidy is reduced as the income rises. Fairly recently a typical Section 235 family of four people had a gross annual income of $6,259, bought an $18,279 house on which it paid $91 a month and received a federal subsidy of $81 a month.

Section 236 is roughly the same for renters of apartments and cooperative housing, except that tenants are expected to pay at least 25 percent of their income as rent. The government pays the rest. In addition, an interest subsidy is paid to the mortgage lender and the project may receive rent-supplement payments for as many as 40 percent of the occupants. A recent computation showed the typical 236 family had three members and an income of $5,303 a year. It paid $115 a month in rent and received a government subsidy of $75 a month.

The 235 and 236 Programs quickly encountered a sea of troubles, only the major ones of which can be described here. The most glaring and publicized pitfall of the program is that it became a speculator's paradise and a grafter's heaven.

A typical example: A speculator would buy an older home in a rundown neighborhood for $3,000. He would then make a few cosmetic repairs to make the property look good, such as shingles and paint on the outside. In the interior he might paint and install a new linoleum floor and tile in the bathroom. A new sink and toilet might be put in. At best he would spend one or two thousand dollars in fixing up the place. Then, he would sell the house for $18,000 to a low income family who had received a 235 mortgage. The speculator would thus pocket a profit of $13,000 on the deal. This sort of thing was done thousands of times with only the numbers changing. The profits were always high.

This is the beginning of the tale, not the end. The tenant moved into his house to find his hopes for home ownership quickly dashed. The roof leaked or the furnace didn't work or the plumbing was bad or the wiring defective. Faced with costly repairs which he could not possibly afford, the new owner moved out after making a few payments, abandoning the house. The federal government became the owner of the vacant property. Vandals quickly did their work and the house had to be boarded up, not a few demolished. Federal taxpayers, of course, continued the mortgage payments on the useless or non-existent house.

This aspect of the 235 Program has been several kinds of a disaster. The situation in Detroit is worst and has received the most publicity. Within two years, 30,000 subsidized houses were sold. About 6,000 were abandoned and repossessed by the government at a loss to the taxpayers of $60 million. Even worse, a subcommittee of the House of Representatives went to the scene to investigate and found the inner city devastated. Entire blocks had been boarded up, vandalized, or gutted by fire. A program designed with the best of intentions to eradicate the slums was incredibly making them worse. And the situation in Detroit was occurring in many other cities.

How did it happen? Primarily, the fault lies with HUD. Departmental officials in the field were supposed to inspect the houses to see that legitimate repairs were made and that the house had been extensively remodeled and was in sound condition before the federally-insured loan was approved. Clearly, this was not done in a significant number of cases.

At best, an excess of zeal caused the shoddy administration of the 235 Program. Historically, HUD had red-lined inner city ghettos as too risky for insured loans. The department literally drew red lines around certain districts where the people were too poor, the houses too decrepit, or the neighborhoods too deteriorated for the government to risk loans. With the coming of the 235 Program, red lining was abandoned as discriminatory. Moreover, directives went out from Washington to relax standards and seek ways to speed up the administrative process so that more low income families could purchase homes. Testimony before Congressional committees indicates that at times HUD field offices engaged in a bit of a race to see how many homes could be sold to poor people. HUD personnel became overworked and inspections became increasingly cursory.

At worst, HUD officials took graft, and the department was rocked by one of the largest scandals in its history. At this writing at least eleven grand jury investigations are going on in major cities. Apparently it was simply too easy for some HUD inspectors to ignore the structural deficiencies in 235 houses in return for a kickback (bribe) from the speculator. There were opportunities for federal officials to speculate themselves or to find other ways to join in the huge profits made at the expense of taxpayers and the poor.

Even if there had been no graft and administrative errors, the 235 Program for older homes carried a high level of risks for the government. Home ownership requires financial discipline and an older home, even if it has been extensively renovated, is more expensive to operate. More money must be spent on maintenance, and low income families simply have less money to spend for that purpose. Their income is often low because they are subject to layoffs, strikes, and other periods of unemployment, yet lack the savings or credit to tide them over such difficult times. Missed mortgage payments and foreclosure can result.

Also, low income families are often easy victims of high pressure salesmen. It takes a bit of sophistication and discipline to resist the "buy now, pay later" importunings of the salesmen of storm windows, shingles, home improvements, dishwashers, freezers, and other exotic appliances. Pride of ownership can sometimes lead the home owner to foreclosure and bankruptcy, if he is not careful.

The construction of new homes and apartments under 235 and 236 Programs also turned into a bonanza for speculators and a nightmare for the HUD and taxpayers. The tales of excessive profiteering, graft, and mismanagement are heard nationwide and some are hair raising. Congressional committees were told of "instant slums," projects built on undesirable sites in such a shoddy manner they were barely inhabitable almost from the outset.

To give one of many possible examples, Dade County, Florida, was the scene of 235 and 236 building projects that were denounced by Miami area newspapers. Reporters talked to owners of the new homes and heard tales of leaky roofs, windows falling out, infestations of flies and other vermin, dried up lawns, rotting wood, faulty plumbing and wiring.

Knowledgeable reporters found the construction in general extraordinarily flimsy with the most minimal plumbing, wiring, heating, and roofing. Experts and residents alike felt the houses would not withstand hurricanes, which are common in Florida. Worse, the homes are of wooden construction rather than cinderblock. If the high winds didn't destroy the houses, termites soon would.

Perhaps the most withering reports were written by Charles Whited in the July 29 and 30, 1971, issues of the *Miami Herald*. The two articles, both included in the record of the House Committee on Banking and Currency, were entitled "A Cash Crop: Instant Houses" and "Cheap Housing, Big Profits?" Some passages:

The big cash crop east of Naranja, in South Dade's Redlands, used to be tomatoes. Now, in more and more of the fields, it's houses. Instant houses. Government-subsidized houses, geared to low income families.

Never mind that the electric wiring is plastic sheathed passed through raw holes drilled in studs and headers—a far cry from the days when you had to run wire through metal conduit.

Forget that the roofing is gravel over two layers of 15-pound asbestos paper mopped with tar, so flimsy that it bulges and buckles in the hot sunshine.

Ignore, if you can, the tub and shower enclosures made of quarter-inch fiberglass. (If you take a shower, don't stamp your feet.)

Disregard the lack of wall insulation, so that your protection against heat and cold consists of low-grade exterior plywood sheeting and an inside covering of half-inch gypsum board.

The price for three bedrooms and two baths in a boxlike house that looks exactly like the neighbors', row after row and street after street, is $21,000.

For in these times of awesome inflation in the construction business with carpenters earning nearly twice as much as schoolteachers and laborers wheeling wheelbarrows for $6 an hour, the suburban crackerbox is making it big. . . .

Naranja, of course, is but one locale. I just happened to visit such a project under construction there Wednesday, in the company of an irate South Dade real estate woman who declared:

"This is ridiculous. Our tax money is creating suburban slums."

And I couldn't help but agree. Even the most maintenance-minded homeowner can only do so much over the years.

Some of the houses I saw, which will be mortgaged for thirty years with government subsidies helping to make the monthly payments, will be lucky to stand half that long—if, indeed, they make it through the next hurricane.

Reporter Whited estimated that the builder made at least $5,000 per house. "Build 100 houses and you've got $500,000 at least," he said, concluding:

> *The irony, however, is that the homebuyer—out of urgent necessity—finds himself locked up on a thirty-year mortgage for a house that can't help but deteriorate rapidly.*
>
> *And if he decides to move, who's going to buy it?*
>
> *It's easy, then, to foresee that in time many of these families will simply abandon their crackerbox homes and strike out for better diggings.*
>
> *Which means the government will simply have to take them back again.*

Critics of subsidized housing maintain that 235 and 236 housing were an expense to Americans other than merely through the taxes to pay for it. The effect of the government programs was to inflate the costs of all types of private home construction. The vast federally subsidized program led builders to expect high profits and created shortages of building materials, land, and labor. The shortages amid high demand are believed to have led to the sharp rise in building costs in 1971 and 1972. Thus, all Americans were affected.

The most shocking unfairness of all was the ability of wealthy investors to make windfall profits off a program intended to aid the poor. Perhaps only tax accountants can fully understand it, but a typical example was cited by analyst James E. Wallace of Abt Associates, Inc., of Cambridge, Massachusetts, in a report to Congress:

> *In a typical 236 rehabilitation project, an investor would give a tax shelter broker $500,000 to invest. The broker keeps $100,000 as his fee and gives $400,000 to the developer. The developer spends $60,000 on the actual housing project and keeps $340,000 as his fee.*

> *In return for his $500,000 investment, the high tax bracket investor has (up to) $200,000 a year taken off his tax (liability) for five years—due to rapid depreciation permitted by the law— and after about twenty years he will sell the project and have the proceeds taxed at the low capital gains rate. In the meantime, the project gets built with a $2 million loan guaranteed by the Federal Housing Administration.*

Another example was provided by writer Gurney Breckenfeld in his *Fortune* magazine article cited earlier:

> *. . . in a typical deal, a group of professionals and businessmen might lay out about $600,000 for a 95 percent interest in a $4,700,000 Section 236 apartment project being built with a $4 million FHA-insured mortgage. The builder-sponsor would pocket most of the $600,000 as his construction profit. Over the next eleven years, provided the project is built at the estimated cost and can be kept reasonably full of tenants, the limited partners should be able to recoup $1,055,000 on their investment, almost entirely in taxes avoided on the members' other income. At the end of that time, if all goes well, the owners might donate the project to charity and acquire a further $1 million in tax deductions.*

The reader need not be an expert in tax laws to grasp the fact that unscrupulous builders and investors, aided by dishonest members of the federal bureaucracy, have engaged in profiteering at the expense of the poor and the taxpayer.

Such shenanigans came with a built-in rationale. The houses might be shoddy, excessive profiteering might be the rule, public officials might be accepting bribes, but the nation's poor people were getting better housing than they had before and perhaps ever hoped to have. Thus, the unscrupulous could convince themselves they were performing humanitarian exercises while bilking the poor and the taxpayers.

It needs to be pointed out that the shady practices were far from universal. Some excellent projects were built at reasonable cost. Yet, there were enough bad apples in the barrel to taint the whole of subsidized housing. *The New York Times* called it "one of the largest housing scandals the FHA has ever seen." The *Times* also called Secretary Romney's actions "unique" among cabinet officers. Instead of trying to hide or whitewash the scandal, he joined the critics of his own department, released internal audits which showed the extent of the malfeasance, and dubbed the whole program a $100 billion "failure." He called for "new approaches" to housing and urban problems.

The scandal in subsidized housing also provoked actions to end, not just the abuses, but the whole program. In January, 1973, President Nixon ordered a freeze on all funds for subsidized housing. This meant the abandonment of many projects then in the planning stage. Finally, in his budget message late in January, the President proposed that the federal government abandon all housing, urban renewal, and model cities programs and turn them over to local governments. The federal role would be to assist in financing the local projects through a $2.3 billion special revenue sharing appropriation. This meant that the federal tax funds would be turned over to local governments in lump sums to be used as they saw fit.

The immediate effect of Mr. Nixon's proposals was to turn the problem back into the lap of Congress. Most observers saw a major debate shaping up over subsidized housing and related issues. Mr. Nixon's proposals would abruptly alter federal policies which had been in operation since the 1930's. Great opposition was anticipated from supporters of public housing and urban redevelopment, along with members of Congress.

The focus for the battle will be the Joint Economic Committee of Congress, chaired by Senator William Proxmire, a Wisconsin Democrat. He has already established a national reputation as a critic of national defense spending. He led the fight in Congress that led to the abandonment of plans to build a supersonic airliner. At this writing, he was expected to be going to take a hard look at federal housing programs. He made this statement:

> *As ranking member of the Housing Subcommittee of the Senate Banking Committee, and as chairman of the Senate Appropriations Subcommittee, which funds housing programs, I intend to pursue the issue of housing programs and housing reform until we get some order out of present chaos.*
>
> *One thing is abundantly clear. Reform of housing programs is long overdue.*
>
> At another point he said that studies showed:
>
> *. . . a crazy-quilt system of too many subsidies, many of which are hidden from budget review, some that provide excessive rates of return to investors, staggering subsidy and housing cost increases, a deficient housing product in far too many cases, and numerous other deficiencies.*

Despite all the criticisms, subsidized housing has its defenders. One defense is that most of the problems and abuses of subsidized housing programs lie in their administration. The idea of subsidized housing is sound. All that is needed is some minor legislative improvements and much better administration by HUD. This was the view set forth in a study prepared by Anthony Downs of the Real Estate Research Corporation of Chicago. His report, now before Congress, was financed by the National Association of Home Builders, the National Association of Mutual Savings Banks, and the United States Savings and Loan League.

Another defense was offered by Roger Starr, executive director of the Citizens Housing and Planning Council in an article in *The*

New York Times of January 28, 1973. He pointed out that subsidized housing counted for 25 percent of the housing starts in 1972. Sudden abandonment of the programs might lead to a serious economic slump in the housing industry and thus the entire economy. He wrote:

> *If the administration frames its program to "get the national government out of housing" or to "clarify the lines of authority" or to "return to the basic principles of a free economic system," the nation will, I'm afraid, pay for this with a serious slowdown in the construction of new housing and the modernization of old housing.*

Mr. Starr also suggested that abandonment of subsidized housing will seriously reduce the amount of decent housing available to lower and middle income families, leaving "the real, live people who need housing . . . [to] grow too old to care." This prognostication quickly became prophetic. Shortly after President Nixon's cutback, the housing industry went into a sharp decline because of a shortage of mortgage money and high interest rates. Late in 1973, Mr. Nixon sought ways to increase housing starts.

Perhaps the most encouraging word on government housing programs came from Secretary Romney as he was leaving HUD. Addressing employees who were rather downcast because they knew many of their functions were about to be axed by the White House, Mr. Romney said:

> *The programs of this department need a searching evaluation, and that evaluation is going to take place almost immediately, and I think you should be aware of that. I don't want you to assume that what may be interpreted as steps backward may not be steps forward over the long run.*

A SEARCH FOR SOLUTIONS— LOWERING THE COSTS

CHAPTER TEN

Housing the poor has proven to be a most stubborn problem to solve. The nation has been working at it for decades, yet millions of Americans still live in substandard, overcrowded, and inadequate dwellings. This simple fact has led to more than a little discouragement, as well as a search for new ways to solve the housing problem.

A starting point for this search is the simple belief that the United States ought to be able to decently house all its citizens. We are most assuredly wealthy enough. We have demonstrated the financial and technical ability not only to land men on the moon, but to provide them a vehicle to ride around in. Surely we ought to be able to develop the technology to erect adequate dwellings for all our people.

If the housing problem is reduced to its bare essentials, it may be said there are only three possible ways to solve it.

1. Raise the poor's income so they can afford better housing.

2. Lower the cost of housing to a level the poor can afford.

3. Some combination of the first two.

Can the cost of housing be lowered? Would it be possible in America of the 1970's to erect new two or three bedroom houses or apartments that could sell for $10,000 or $15,000? This would make it possible for all but the very poorest to afford them. Yet, such a goal seems as far out of reach as the old alchemist's dream of turning lead into gold.

Such low-cost housing seems impossible as long as conventional building methods and materials are used. There seems to be no way that workmen cutting and hammering and mortaring and wiring and painting can bring the costs down to the level people can afford.

But there is hope (or perhaps optimism) that eventually technology and mass production techniques can accomplish what conventional builders cannot. The Department of Housing and Urban Development launched "Operation Breakthrough" in 1969 aimed at developing factory-built "modular" homes. The idea is simple. Instead of building homes or apartment houses on the site, the structures would be built in factories as separate parts of the whole. These parts or modules would be transported to the site to be fitted together into a house or apartment building. It makes sense to proponents of the system that mass produced kitchens, bathrooms, or bedrooms just have to be cheaper than individually constructed ones.

Operation Breakthrough earned many plaudits. It seemed an application of "Yankee ingenuity" to the housing problem. A whole new industry was envisioned.

By 1972, some of the optimism had given way to discouragement. Scores of companies entered the field, including some large ones such as the Aluminum Company of America, General Electric, International Telephone and Telegraph, and Republic Steel. But many companies lost a great deal of money. It seemed there were technical problems in the construction. The cost of transporting the modules from the factory to the site more than offset the economies of construction. Indeed, with few exceptions, modular homes and apartments cost more than conventionally built structures.

Proponents of modular construction remain cautiously optimistic, however. It is believed greater profits will occur when the number of companies in the industry is reduced. There are simply too many manufacturers for all to make money. Transportation costs can be reduced when factories are located in areas of great potential demand. Other savings could be made by cutting red tape so the modules roll off the assembly line and go right to the building site, rather than being stacked up in company warehouses. Local building codes need to be revised to permit the new techniques to be used.

In short, modular housing is a new industry with all the growing pains of any new industry. It is believed that with time and better methods, the cost of home construction can be lowered. But how low? The mobile home portion of the industry now sells units for under $15,000, offering hope that more conventional housing could be built for a similar price. Best of all, modular housing offers a chance, at least, that a great many housing units can be built rather quickly. This is important to any solution to the housing problem.

The examination of the costs of housing has led to widespread disenchantment with one of the big ideas of the 1950's and 1960's—rehabilitation. America's cities contain large numbers of dwellings which are structurally sound, but need to be repaired and remodeled. It seemed logical that older buildings could be rehabilitated more quickly and more economically than new housing could be built. After a decade of effort, this idea has exploded into a myth. Rehabilitation is slow and expensive. Final costs do not end up something the poor can afford. Worse, many of the poor want new housing, not a patch up job. The old homes and apartments have built-in inconveniences which no amount of rehabilitation will erase.

Many experts believe the inner city housing problem will be solved not by philanthropy but by the profit motive. Some way must be found to enlist private capital—and a great deal of it—into low-cost housing construction.

The basis for this idea is that Americans have shown they can perform production and economic miracles when a profit is involved. Consider cars, telephones, television sets, and a host of other gadgets. If this same energy and motivation could be applied to slum clearance, America would become a housing paradise within a decade.

Another basis for this approach is the proverbial "law of supply and demand" in economics. There is a large demand for new, low-cost housing and a short supply of it. It would just seem that, inevitably, profit-minded businessmen would find a way to meet that demand and make a lot of money out of it. Something similar to this happened in the years following World War II when millions of homes and apartments were built for middle and upper income families.

But the idea or the dream has simply remained that. Low-cost housing, as an act of private enterprise, remains much less profitable than middle and upper income housing, if not a money losing proposition altogether.

What would it take to make the dream of privately built and financed low-cost housing come true? It may well be impossible, but the notion persists among housing experts that it could come true more easily than anyone thinks.

For starters, what is needed is for very large companies to enter the field. Housing is almost entirely provided by small companies that simply do not have the financing or management expertise to build on a truly large scale. To be made profitable, low-cost housing must be built by the tens of thousands of units over a very large area. What is needed is a General Motors, Ford, American Telephone and Telegraph, General Electric, or some other economic colossus. Such a large company would have the borrowing power, the management know-how, the money to finance technological research into new construction techniques, and the economic strength to reduce its profits per housing unit to a very low amount, yet make money because it builds a great many of them.

Let's try to envision this as a hypothetical exercise. Suppose Behemoth Builders, Inc., a giant company with multi-billion dollar assets, undertook to rebuild the South Bronx slum of New York City. It planned to build a hundred thousand housing units in six basic designs using its newly-developed material, "rockhard," a form of space age plastic. Behemoth can cut the cost of the material by a third by building a factory to manufacture it right on the spot. The factory will be dismantled and moved to a new site when the project is completed. Behemoth plans to make an average 1 percent profit on all housing units. It will, of course, make more money on all stores, factories, office buildings, and other commercial facilities built in the South Bronx. First units are expected to be ready for occupancy in a year. There is a regular schedule of demolition and construction over a ten-year period.

Is this a pipedream? It may well be. No such immense corporation exists and the fiscal difficulties of housing construction are such that there may be no way costs could be lowered enough to make such a harebrained scheme feasible—without government help.

If this is so, then what type of government help? The tendency is to think in terms of the kind of local, state, and federal aid that has been dispensed in the past. One, as we have seen, is government-insured loans now used in public housing projects, or FHA loans. Banks, insurance companies, and other lending institutions can take greater risks in lending money because they know the federal government stands behind the loans. Second, government simply lends the money out of the treasury. Third, the government agrees to pay back the principle and interest over forty years or more. Fourth, the government agrees to pay part of the interest on the borrowed money so that the builder would have to pay only 1 or 2 percent interest on his capital. All of these are forms of slum clearance subsidies. And, President Nixon is talking about abandoning the lot of them.

Another form of government aid in existence is tax relief. The builder pays the full cost of construction, but is granted a form of subsidy after the fact in the form of tax relief. Perhaps he is permitted to deduct the full cost of his interest payments for building low-cost housing, or he is permitted a very fast write off of depreciation (the building might be depreciated in ten years instead of fifty) to offset taxes on his profits, or he is simply granted a flat deduction for building low-cost housing. Local governments could subsidize such construction by granting relief from local property taxes, such as taxing at a lower rate or exempting the buildings from taxation for a period of years.

Still another form of aid is for government to assume part of the cost of construction. Since land costs are one of the biggest items in any project, governments can buy the land and clear it, then sell it to a private developer for an amount considerably below the cost. This form of subsidy, widely used for many years, is called urban renewal. Governments can also aid private builders by assuming the costs of such project appurtenances as parks, playgrounds, schools, streets, highways, and utilities.

To repeat, all of these forms of subsidy have been in use and all have been found wanting or inadequate. President Nixon proposed early in 1973 to curtail or abandon most of them as far too expensive for the gain that resulted.

One bold and money-saving step local governments could take to aid developers would be to cut the red tape now involved in any sort of urban redevelopment. Indeed, there probably can be no real progress in housing development until the process is vastly simplified.

As it now stands, housing developers must obtain hundreds, perhaps thousands, of permissions from various levels of government. Bevies of officials must be consulted in such areas as highways, traffic, schools, parks, sewers, water, and many others. State, federal, and local inspectors appear in droves. Plans must be prepared in quadruplicate and submitted to scores of officials, none of whom are in a hurry. Hundreds of laws governing zoning, building codes, fire regulations, and the like must be consulted. Public meetings must be held with seemingly innumerable citizens groups. A builder must spend a rather sizeable fortune on architects, planners, draftsmen, and lawyers (not to mention under-the-table graft to unscrupulous officials) before he ever buys a parcel of land or sticks a spade in the earth. This expenditure not only adds to the cost, but it sometimes delays the project for years. Potential developers are exasperated and driven away.

Could the whole process be simplified? Surely it could. Consider what would happen if a major city such as New York, Chicago, or San Francisco were to be leveled by a natural disaster such as an earthquake or tidal wave. Surely local officials, faced with a gargantuan rebuilding task would find a way to dispense with the bureaucratic red tape so that builders could get on with the necessary construction. But a natural disaster is not always required before a job can be accomplished. In the mid-1950's, the city of Baltimore was buffeted by traffic problems that were about the worst in the nation. Finally at the point of exasperation, city officials hired the best man in the country, the late Henry A. Barnes, gave him ample funds, and, best of all, nearly autocratic authority to do whatever he felt necessary to improve traffic in the city. In a rather short time, he performed a small miracle.

Something similar may have to occur in low-cost housing. One man may need to be given sufficient authority to cut through the maze of red tape, bearing responsibility to see that the job is done quickly and efficiently. Such an action would save the local governments a great deal of money spent on the scores of boards, commissions, and bureaus that have a hand in housing. It would also be a form of subsidy to private builders who would find their tasks cheaper and far easier.

This question of lowering the cost of housing cannot be left without a brief discussion of a truly pie-in-the-sky notion. Could any way or ways be found to reduce the truly tremendous cost of land acquisition for urban redevelopment? If it could, low-cost housing would soon follow. As it is now, much of urban land is owned by extremely wealthy individuals, foundations, and trusts.* On the land are large numbers of tenements, many of them abandoned. The buildings themselves are of relatively little value, yet

---

* Columbia University in New York City reportedly owns a significant portion of Harlem, having received it as gifts from donors.

the land is considered immensely valuable. The developer, whether using tax dollars or private funds, pays a high, high price for it, slum though it may be.

In the United States, land may not be confiscated by the government without proper payment to the owner. But would it be possible for government, using its zoning and similar powers, to require that owners of land bear a responsibility to maintain a certain standard of the use of the land; that is, not rat infested tenements but decent low-cost housing?

Perhaps ways could be found to encourage owners of slum land to participate in low-cost housing projects. For example, land owners might be persuaded (perhaps even required) to accept shares of dividend-paying stock in the project or the building company in lieu of cash payment for their land. Such financial devices are common in private business, but have not been tried in city rebuilding.

In summary, there would seem to be many plans and approaches to low-cost housing which have not yet been tried. Americans seem to be looking at slum clearance as a philanthropic exercise, rather than as a means of making money, as a matter for the government to take care of rather than as something the people can do themselves.

A SEARCH FOR SOLUTIONS—RAISING INCOMES

CHAPTER ELEVEN

Raise the income of the poor so they can afford to buy or rent better housing. That would seem a feasible way to solve the housing problem.

Feasible, perhaps, but also very difficult. The United States has been trying to enrich the poor just about as long as it has been trying to provide public housing. This country dispenses billions of dollars yearly in various forms of public welfare, social security, medical care, health clinics, job training, food stamps, educational and other programs aimed at aiding the poor. Much of the aid is direct in the form of cash placed in the hands of the poor family. The rest is indirect aid to take the place of cash (free health clinics or food stamps, for example) or a means by which the poor can increase their earnings (job training).

It is an error to suggest that these programs have failed. They have kept millions of people from hunger and not a few from starvation. The incidence of disease has been lowered. Many have used these forms of aid to rise from poverty. A celebrated example at this writing is George Foreman, the heavyweight boxing champion in 1973. He got his start with the federal Job Corps.

And yet, there is a widespread feeling that the government programs to enrich the poor have been a failure. The most pronounced evidence is the continued existence of ten to twenty million poor people, living in bad housing in teeming ghettos or rural pestholes amid disease, crime, folly, and futility. Poverty has always been with us and it remains, seemingly eradicable, despite the many billions spent annually to combat it. National discouragement with the problem is certainly understandable.

This is a book on housing, not on poverty, but the housing problem is the child of poverty. Bad housing exists largely because the people in it cannot afford any better. If they could, they would move into it. In that sense, impoverished Americans are not an iota different from middle or upper income Americans. Our housing reflects our economic station in life.

We could solve the housing problem by solving the poverty problem. Everyone knows this. But our efforts against poverty have been crippled by some myths we carry around. The first is that poverty is a temporary condition. Lots of people get down on their luck but by hard work, discipline, scrimping, saving, doing without for a while, they will climb out of the pit of poverty and thereby have their character ennobled by their courageous effort.

This is certainly a common American experience, much glorified in story and movie. But we really ought to realize that it was far from a universal experience. Many of those people who went west in the covered wagons to seek their fortunes, simply died in unmarked graves by the wayside. And many others who stayed behind in the teeming slums, died there in poverty. And many who lived in sod houses in the prairie and grubbed at a homestead died in those sod houses and lost the farms to the big ranchers.

America has always had a sizeable middle class, but it has also always had a sizeable poor class. In fact, poverty is as American as apple pie. It is only fairly recently, on the order of the last thirty years, that the United States has had much experience with widespread affluence. We have succeeded in reducing the number of poor people, but we have not eliminated the condition.

We move a little closer to solving the poverty problem when we realize that the poor have always been among us. We have a *chronic,* not a temporary problem. There are black people in the United States whose families have known nothing but abject poverty since their original ancestors were led off the slave ships in chains. And, when poverty exists generation upon generation it does things to people, their aspirations, their strength, their will, their use of their native intelligence, even their morality. We are only now realizing the importance of the simple fact that the black poor speak a dialect known as "black English." Never having spoken regular English, it is difficult for them to learn to read it.

A second myth is that the poor are lazy. If only they would

work, like the rest of Americans, they could rise from poverty, buy houses, and enjoy the fabled American affluence. In their laziness, the poor would rather live off of welfare and other public payments. The working man is in fact impoverished by the taxes he pays to support the shiftless poor. If welfare and other payments were stopped and the poor starved a little, they might go to work, too.

This myth is a form of cruelty, for it subsists on the fraudulent notion that there are "plenty" of jobs for the poor and ignores the undeniable fact that the jobs that are available do not pay enough to raise the person out of poverty. In their article "Crisis of the Underemployed" (referred to earlier), authors William Spring, Bennett Harrison, and Thomas Vietorisz pointed out:

> *Most Americans continue to believe (as they have been taught to believe) that there are enough "good jobs" in the economy to go around if a man really wants to work. What the blue-collar worker does not understand is that however hard-pressed he may be by taxes and the rising cost of living, labor-market conditions for the poor are much worse. The high rates of subemployment reveal a sharp division between conditions in what a growing number of young economists refer to as the "primary labor market," where unionized, relatively well-paying, stable jobs are available, and a "secondary labor market" in the inner city, characterized by low wages, unstable opportunities for work, and the absence of unions.*

The plight of the inner cities is that too many of the good, first class employers have moved out. The jobs that are left are too often menial, temporary, low paying, and all too few. To tell the poor to get a job and work instead of accepting welfare is to tell him, all too often, to flap his arms and deliver the air mail.

The third myth is that the poor are penniless. Far from it. They have money. They just don't have enough of it or, too often, don't spend what they have wisely (or, better said, they don't spend their money any more wisely than the rest of the population). The trouble is, the poor need to spend their wages with the proverbial acumen of Solomon. In aggregate the poor have a lot of money and the shills, scalpers, and unscrupulous, dedicated to skinning them out of it, descend on the ghettos like locusts. The poor, in their helplessness, are overcharged for food, housing, furniture, appliances, and just about everything else. They are victimized by loan sharks, landlords, businessmen of wide variety, crooks—and even the purveyors of state lottery tickets. Those, and they are legion, who prey on the poor for profit do not cause the poverty, but they worsen it and keep the poor entrapped in it longer. Much of the tax money the nation gives to the poor does not benefit the poor so much as it enriches the businessmen, landlords, loan companies, and out-and-out crooks who leech from the indigent.

The traditional American approach to aiding the poor is through welfare payments. The apex of liberal thought in the 1970's is to provide every American family with some form of "guaranteed annual income," perhaps through direct payment or through some form of negative income tax. President Nixon proposed such a plan in 1969, then became disenchanted with the scheme, and by 1972 had abandoned it in favor of the work ethic. Middle class Americans are opposed to welfare both on philosophic grounds and a belief that outright grants do not and will not work. By 1973, passage of the guaranteed annual income plan in Congress was deemed impossible.

In any event, no one is talking about guaranteeing the poor enough income to solve the housing problem. Mr. Nixon proposed a floor of $2,400 with subsidies for the working poor up to about $4,300. The most money advocates of the income plan were talking about was $6,500 a year for a family of four. This would not buy a house at today's prices.

Public welfare or a guaranteed income became a major issue in the 1972 Presidential election campaign. President Nixon, who opposed handouts and favored work over welfare, won 60 percent of the vote and a landslide victory. Unfortunately, all the attention paid to the various welfare plans obscured other, perhaps more viable ways to alleviate poverty.

Search could begin for ways to increase the earnings of the millions of poor who work. The legal minimum wage in the United States is $1.60 an hour, set in 1966. If it had been raised to keep pace with inflation, it would have been $2.06 an hour in 1972. Clearly, simply raising the minimum wage to $2 or $2.50 an hour would help reduce poverty. Congress passed a bill raising the minimum wage, but President Nixon vetoed it.

Such a suggestion encounters immediate objection. Many firms cannot afford to pay such wages—or claim they can't. The fear is that many employers will go out of business if forced to pay higher wages and the result will be less, not more jobs in ghettos. Perhaps this is so, but it surely seems a contention that ought to be studied, rather than simply taken for granted.

Another approach to combating poverty, rather than through outright grants of money, is to increase the number of public service jobs. There are many tasks that need to be done in America. Men and women could be put to work doing them. Examples: The mails in the United States are notoriously slow and getting slower. Millions of jobs could be created in the Postal Service simply by increasing deliveries to twice a day. There are shortages of policemen, firemen, teachers aides, nurses aides, library assistants, sanitation men, street cleaners, and park employees. There are nearly endless tasks in cleaning up pollution, protecting the environment, and beautifying our highways and parks. A full list, if not endless, is long.*

* It is perhaps an exercise in longing for the "good old days," but various practices of the past did have the virtue of making more jobs and relieving

Employing the poor and near poor at such tasks would require no small sum of tax money. Several billion dollars would have to be spent annually. But the expenditure would reduce welfare and similar payments, help reduce poverty, and lessen the housing and other related problems, as well as aid the nation and the quality of life in it. It seems a method of reducing poverty to be preferred over handouts which do little or no good for anyone, including the poor. But, President Nixon, who has strongly advocated that the poor work (apparently at nonexistent jobs), vetoed a plan in 1970 to have the federal government spend $4.5 billion over a three-year period to finance public service employment. In 1971, a $1 billion plan, enough to provide 180,000 jobs, was implemented under the Emergency Employment Act. It has proved popular with state and local officials and has seemed easy to administer.

It is fantasy, however, to assume that even the most ambitious of such programs could eliminate poverty entirely. The ranks of the poor include millions who are simply unemployable—children, the elderly, mothers of young children, and people who are physically or mentally incapacitated. Such unfortunates are going to have to be supported entirely or in part at taxpayers' expense into the conceivable future—that is, unless there are sizeable increases in private charity or we issue licenses to starve.

There are other ways to increase the ability of the poor and near poor to buy property. A change in federal income tax laws could greatly aid lower income families. As now written, the law permits home owners to deduct from their income all property taxes and in-

poverty. Remember the days when there was a conductor or ticket taker on public buses, when there were parking attendants instead of impersonal meters, when there were handymen to make minor repairs and garden. Our age of automated turnstiles, banking machines, and the like may have advantages. They may increase the demand for skilled labor, but they also diminish the need for unskilled labor. Taxes to fight poverty, crime, and other urban ills are increased because of the gradual disappearance of unskilled or semi-skilled jobs. Progress bears its price.

terest payments on the mortgage. There are other provisions for loss due to fire, natural causes, or theft. If the house is sold, the profit is not taxed if it is immediately invested in another personal dwelling. These are significant subsidies to home owners and even more so to banks and other lending institutions, the home construction industry, and the real estate business.

Those who rent, and that includes the bulk of the lower income families, receive no such tax deductions. Through their rent, low income families indirectly pay local property taxes and make interest payments, yet no deduction is possible. If lower income families were allowed to deduct some portion of their rent, this would make more money available to them. It would also encourage them to pay higher rent for better properties, for the higher the rent the greater the tax savings. It is honestly difficult to understand why Congress does not take this rather simple step as a means of combating the housing problem. It would be a form of housing subsidy far easier to administer than that used under the 236 Program.

There is also talk of housing "allowances" as a means of aiding the poor. Secretary Romney said he favored such a system before leaving office, but refused to specify what he had in mind.

The theoretical advantages of allowances are obvious. Instead of a state or federal government getting involved in planning, financing, and building low-cost housing, it would simply give the indigent family money to spend as it saw fit in the housing market. The availability of such allowances in the ghetto would presumably stimulate private builders to erect more low-cost housing.

In the absence of a concrete plan at this writing, it must be speculated that Mr. Romney's allowances would work in one of two ways, either as a lump sum to form the down payment on a dwelling or a monthly stipend to defray housing costs. Several state and local governments, including New York City, now include housing allowances in their welfare payments.

It is not difficult to foresee that such a program would encounter the same opposition as welfare payments do. Those who have worked and struggled to buy a house simply object to having one given to those who did not earn it. Perhaps if a greater effort were made to explain to home owners that the tax deductions are a form of on-going subsidy to them, then they might not object so much to allowances as a form of subsidy to those who do not now receive any.

If one or all of these methods—allowances, tax subsidies, public service jobs, higher minimum wages, or guaranteed incomes— were used successfully to reduce poverty, what would be the effect on the housing problem? Would bad housing simply go away from whence it came? Oh, that it were so, but only the naïve can really believe it.

For openers, the considerable number of hard core unemployables will probably always require public housing much in the manner that it now exists. But successful work programs could siphon off many of the near poor* families into the regular housing market.

Their first action in all but the rarest instances will be to move out of the ghetto, whether it be located in an urban, small town, or rural setting. If they are black, Indian, Puerto Rican, or member of some other minority, they may encounter prejudice. But if they have the dollars they will find a community somewhere offering improved protection, education, and opportunity.

It is therefore not difficult to conceive—if anti-poverty programs are successful—of an intensification of the flight to the suburbs, of the urban ghettos becoming increasingly abandoned and more

---

* One must suffer in search of terminology. Such phrases as "upper lower income" or "lower middle income" or "affluent poor" come to mind. Amid such options, the term "near poor" seems the least of the evils. In any event, I am speaking of families of four with incomes of $6,000 to $8,000. Larger families can make twice those amounts and still be poor.

than ever inhabited by the hard core poor and by the criminals, addicts, drunks, and others of life's losers. We may then end up not with slum clearance or urban redevelopment, but an intensification of the very problems which now buffet America's cities.

In his series of soul-searching speeches with which Secretary Romney closed out his four years in office, he identified the crisis of the American city as one of loss of function. Most inner cities are no longer very good places to live. Most employment is found on the fringes of cities, not downtown. The jobs that exist in the ghettos tend to be menial and low paying. Purchases are now more commonly made in suburban shopping centers. Many cities are now building their athletic stadiums out of the center of town. Colleges and universities have erected suburban campuses. Churches long ago followed their congregations to the country. Many downtowns have lost a great deal of their pre-eminence as cultural, recreational, and entertainment centers.

A casual glance at the business district of most American cities would seem to indicate that Mr. Romney is exaggerating. In the last decade the skylines of most American cities has changed. Using the urban renewal process, cities have erected modern office buildings, hotels, luxury apartments, civic auditoriums, and attractive parks and plazas. Mr. Romney's lamentation of the loss of inner city function would seem not quite to square with the hustling prosperity of Manhattan or The Loop in Chicago or the architectural transformations in Hartford, Boston, Philadelphia, Baltimore, Atlanta, Houston, St. Louis, Denver, Detroit, or San Francisco. As a means of rebuilding the hubs of cities, urban renewal has been a great success.

The American city may be likened to a wheel. There is a small downtown hub, a pocket of prosperity. On the rim are the suburbs, prosperous with housing and shopping centers and factories and much of the substance of life. The hub and the rim are joined by the spokes—expressways linking downtown to the suburbs. In between lie the great, gray, festering ghettos or other areas of older homes threatened by blight.

The loss of function of which Mr. Romney spoke is that the ghettos seem to serve no useful purpose in modern society. Also, the downtown hub cannot economically support the ghetto population. The shiny new office buildings do not offer enough jobs or the right kind of jobs to relieve the poverty of the ghettos. The tax burden for education, welfare, crime control, and other services in the ghetto is more than the commercial hub can bear. And the suburbs won't help. Most of them are politically independent. They raise their own taxes and apply them to their own problems, which are relatively few.

The central issue in all urban problems, including housing, is how to get the affluent suburbs to help pay for the vitally needed improvements in the inner city. It is this we take up in the final chapter.

A CONSERVATIVE REVOLUTION?

CHAPTER TWELVE

Early in February, 1973, an elderly man parked his new Buick in front of his $50,000 home in a fashionable northwest section of Washington, D.C. As he reached in the back seat to pick up his overcoat and briefcase, two young men came up to him, grabbed his wallet, watch, and gold Phi Beta Kappa key. Although he apparently did not resist, one of the thugs struck him and the other said, "Now we're going to shoot you." Senator John Stennis of Mississippi fell gravely wounded.

The entire nation was shocked by a seemingly senseless crime. A distinguished senator known for his dedication to his legislative duties and unfailing courtesy was gunned down in front of his home. Police said there was apparently no political motive for the crime. It was just a mugging and robbery. The perpetrators had no idea of the identity of their victim, except that he looked prosperous.

The crime was all the more shocking because it occurred in a posh neighborhood where such crimes, common in the ghetto, are not supposed to happen. The attack on Senator Stennis serves to illustrate, however, that the suburbs, no matter how wealthy, do not have immunity from the problems which afflict the inner city.

Every writer and observer on urban affairs has lamented the "balkanization" of our cities. That word describes the division of metropolitan areas into scores of autonomous political divisions—various authority vested in the state, the city, or the town, plus independent districts for schools, water, sewage, transit, and many more. To form a concerted attack on almost any urban problem, including housing, is to seek agreement among the political units that are exasperatingly divided. They cannot agree on what the problem is, let alone how to solve it.

The suburbs exist to protect their residents. This means keeping out the poor and the socially "unfit." The suburbanites pay the high cost in money and in the inconvenience of living in the outskirts simply to escape the crime, disease, and other problems of the inner city. They want good schools and are generally prepared to pay for them. They are not about to pay for support of the poor or for services that benefit the poor. As we have seen, the wealth of the metropolitan area has been drained off into the suburbs, leaving the city proper strapped for funds to take care of the poor.

Yet, the affluent residents of the suburbs cannot escape what happens in the ghettos. They breathe the same polluted air. If there is a shortage of water and sewage capacity, chances are both the affluent and the indigent are affected. Both are caught in the same traffic jams. Drug addiction that began in the ghetto has spread to the suburbs to strike the children of middle class parents. Crime, as the assault on Senator Stennis demonstrates, will just not confine itself to "where it belongs."

Nevertheless, to suggest to the residents of most suburbs that they voluntarily tax themselves and turn the money over to the central city to improve housing, education, and social services in the ghetto would be a waste of breath. "It's not our problem," they say, although actually, the affluent in the suburbs have been paying for the costs of the ghetto for some time, although few have thought of it as such. The federal (and to a lesser extent state) governments have collected taxes, in the form of levies on incomes, from suburban residents and turned them over to city governments as various forms of aid to the poor.

For rather obvious reasons, the federal lawmakers have not declared themselves Robin Hood, taking from the rich to give to the poor, but they have over the years erected a complicated mechanism to accomplish the same purpose. The formal name for the device is "grants in aid." Under various formulae, the federal government has dispensed tax money for housing, health, education, and other purposes. Perhaps to make the process less obvious and more democratic, aid has also been given to a host of less than needy citizens, such as farmers, defense contractors, transportation companies, the well-to-do elderly (and through tax shelters just about anyone earning more than $50,000 a year).

At approximately the same time as the assault on Senator Stennis, President Nixon proposed a major alteration of this process. He sent to Congress his Fiscal 1974 budget, his proposal for spending between July 1, 1973 and June 30, 1974. The budget he sent to Congress proposed to eliminate or reduce the appropriation for more than one hundred federal programs, including housing, which had previously been deemed of social benefit to Americans.

Mr. Nixon explained that he wanted to hold the line on spending, lest it lead to higher taxes and/or higher prices and inflation that would damage the economy. Moreover, he expressed his philosophical belief that "throwing money at problems" does not solve them. "If we were to continue to expand the Federal Government at the rate of the past several decades, it would soon consume us entirely." He said that ill-conceived federal programs have "deceived our people because many of the intended beneficiaries received far less than was promised, thus undermining public faith in the effectiveness of government as a whole." He suggested that the answer to domestic problems is "less waste, more results, and greater freedom for the individual American to earn a rightful place in his own community."

The President made clear his intention to phase out many of the costly federal social programs and turn the functions over to the state and local governments, using revenue sharing of federal taxes to help finance them. He stated his belief that such methods would reduce the federal bureaucracy and give local residents greater control over how the money is spent.

Mr. Nixon, an avowed middle-of-the-road conservative, espousing conservative position, was nonetheless offering a revolutionary idea. The United States has never really had state and local social programs. Federal programs came into existence in the 1930's largely because of the ineptness and inability of state and local governments to provide for the jobless, homeless, and hungry in the Great Depression. Programs such as housing and welfare, which are administered at the local level, are largely financed by the federal government and operate in accordance with federal regulations. If the federal role were disbanded or greatly diminished, it would surely call for great changes in state and local governments and the way they are operated.

If Congress adopts the President's plan, what might be the results? A smaller federal bureaucracy, for one. The need for a Department of Housing and Urban Development and of Health, Education, and Welfare would seem greatly diminished; indeed, both might well be superfluous.

Second, a degree of national uniformity would be lost. It must be assumed that some local governments would use their lump sum federal revenues to build low-cost housing, fight crime, and combat other social ills, while some localities would use the funds to erect public monuments or perhaps even reduce local taxes.

The loss of uniformity would cause instant difficulties for those cities or states which invested the federal revenues in low-cost housing. There is a law of effect at work. As soon as any public improvement is made it tends to become self defeating through overuse. As soon as a new highway is opened or an improved traffic pattern established, motorists quickly use it and the new facility becomes overcrowded. It is predictable that those cities which invest in low-cost housing and other social improvements will have an immigration of poor people from other areas. The new housing will quickly fill up and a new burden will fall on the city's social services.

At present federal housing aid is spread over all states and most communities. A high degree of uniformity results, offering at least a semblance of equal opportunity for all people in need of better housing.

A third result of President Nixon's proposals would be a reduction in the amounts affluent suburbs now pay for inner city housing and other social problems. The general revenue sharing which went into effect in 1972 resulted in windfalls for many suburban communities that really didn't need the money. Many of the towns used the money to reduce local property taxes or at least to avoid increasing them. There were some expenditures for rather needless frills, such as Christmas decorations. Big city mayors, hearing of the President's plan for special revenue sharing to replace existing grants-in-aid, said they would get less federal money under the proposed system.

A fourth possible result is that the President's ideas could work. With the spigot of federal housing appropriations turned off, it is possible that local governments might make greater efforts or that private industry might be stimulated to make larger investments— or both.

There are two programs now in existence which offer some grounds for optimism that the President's ideas might work. One is New York State's Urban Development Corporation (UDC) headed by Edward J. Logue. It is perhaps the nation's most successful state housing authority. Many consider it a model for the nation. Under its state charter, the UDC has authority not merely to finance mortgages, but to move into any community in the state, condemn property, raze anything standing on it, and redevelop with anything UDC wants to build, including institutional, commercial, or industrial buildings. In the process, UDC can override local building codes, zoning laws and, if necessary, even public sentiment. The UDC has $1.5 billion in borrowing power granted by the state. By November, 1972, it had completed thirteen projects housing 7,000 persons and broken ground on fifty-two more. An additional fifty-one were in the planning stages. The freeze on federal subsidies, of course, threatened the latter projects.

Mr. Logue, the corporation president, has vast experience in public housing, coming to his job from New Haven, Connecticut, and Boston. He is highly energetic, and has a talent for wielding his agency's great powers with an awareness of political realities. He has managed to keep voter antipathy to his site selections to a minimum.

No one knows for certain, but there are federal officials who believe that when Mr. Nixon speaks of returning housing programs to local control, he has in mind agencies such as that in New York State, legally powerful, well-financed, and ably led.

Another highly regarded approach is the Hartford Process. It attempts to blend public and private capital to rebuild and enrich the quality of life in the area surrounding Hartford, Connecticut. This is to be accomplished through two nonprofit public service corporations: The Greater Hartford Process, Inc., is to "examine the region, set forth the goals and the arithmetic for a better region, and design specific proposals to bring about a region that 'works.' " The Greater Hartford Community Development Corporation ("DevCo") "will obtain financing, acquire land, and engage in site planning, development and management of the community development proposals suggested by Process and appropriately approved by the residents of the region."

The boards of directors of both corporations are studded with representatives of a full spectrum of regional life, including business, labor, residents, local government, and planning agencies. The aim is to attack local problems comprehensively on a metropolitan and regional basis, rather than piecemeal. For example, housing projects would be tied in with employment, transportation, education, and other requirements for a viable community. Citizens will participate in the process from its inception.

The optimist can believe that President Nixon's proposals will encourage programs such as those in New York State or Hartford. The pessimist can believe that a pattern of massive neglect could result from the White House proposals in which urban problems worsen until the poor react with a new outbreak of rage and rioting.

It is very clear that the nation has arrived at a crossroads (if not a crisis) in its efforts to house the poor. The methods that have been used in the past have been declared a failure, perhaps unfairly. President Nixon has placed the prestige of his office behind a plan to abolish many of the housing programs and to diminish the federal role in housing. The immediate result was a sharp depression of the housing industry. A combination of high prices, high interest rates, and scarce mortgage money reduced buyer interest in new homes. The entire home construction industry was adversely affected.

Another result has been a confrontation with the Democratic Party and the United States Congress, which authored the existing programs. President Nixon, at this writing, had frozen existing programs and impounded the funds. He has stated that he will veto any new programs with which he disagrees and refuse to spend any appropriations. A constitutional crisis between the President and Congress has been joined.

Unfortunately, even tragically, a dialogue leading toward new direction in solving America's housing problems was interrupted by Watergate, the massive, unprecedented political scandals of the Nixon administration. Allegations of such illegal and immoral acts as burglary, wiretapping, obstruction of justice, perjury, subornation of perjury, solicitation of illegal campaign funds, bribery, and conspiracy to commit such acts stunned the White House staff. There were many resignations in Mr. Nixon's administration. The House of Representatives began an investigation to determine if the President should be impeached.

The Watergate scandal led to a huge decline in Mr. Nixon's popularity and prestige. The Watergate affairs and their repercussions absorbed the nation, most particularly Congress and Mr. Nixon. Housing was one of many national problems which was neglected as the United States suffered a crisis of leadership.

These gross difficulties were exacerbated by the fuel shortage, or "energy crisis" as it was called. The home construction industry, already depressed by high interest rates, a shortage of money for mortgages, and other economic conditions, was hard hit. There were fears that the housing industry might remain depressed until some questions were answered: How long would the fuel shortage remain? And how serious would it be? Would the shortage of fuels for transportation, heating, and electricity cause a drastic change in the life-styles of Americans? Specifically, would new types of homes be built? Would the energy-wasting extravagances of suburbia have to be sacrificed for a more compact urban society?

One answer seems clear. The housing problems seem likely to remain a constant in American life, affecting the affluent, middle class, and poor alike. To make our goal of a decent, comfortable dwelling place for all citizens possible will require a high level of intelligence, good will, and human energy in the years ahead. I hope you will participate.

Foote, Nelson N., Janet Abu-lughod, Mary Mix Foley, and Louis Winnick. *Housing Choices and Housing Constraints*. New York: McGraw-Hill, 1960.

Friedman, Lawrence M. *Government and Slum Housing*. Chicago: Rand McNally Co., 1968.

Glazer, Nathan and David McEntire. *Studies in Housing and Minority Groups*. Berkeley, Calif.: University of California Press, 1960.

Haring, Joseph E., ed. *Urban and Regional Economics*. Boston: Houghton Mifflin Co., 1972.

Harrington, Michael. *The Other America*. New York: Macmillan Co., 1963.

Harris, Fred R. and John V. Lindsay. *The State of the Cities: Report of the Commission on Cities in the 1970's*. New York: Praeger, 1972.

Jacobs, Jane. *The Death and Life of Great American Cities*. New York: Random House, 1961.

Keats, John. *The Crack in the Picture Window*. Boston: Houghton Mifflin Co., 1956.

Liston, Robert A. *The American Poor*. New York: Delacorte Press, 1970.

Riis, Jacob A. *The Battle with the Slums*. New York: Macmillan Co., 1912.

Schreiber, Arthur F., Paul K. Gatons, and Richard B. Clemmer, eds. *Economics of Urban Problems: An Introduction*. Boston: Houghton Mifflin Co., 1971.

———. *Economics of Urban Problems: Selected Readings*. Boston: Houghton Mifflin Co., 1972.

Seligman, Ben P. *Permanent Poverty*. Chicago: Quadrangle Books, 1968.

Wilson, James Q., ed. *Urban Renewal: The Record and the Controversy*. Cambridge, Mass.: MIT Press, 1966.

SELECTED READING

INDEX

Robert A. Liston was born in Youngstown, Ohio. He received his B.A. from Hiram College in Ohio where he majored in history and political science. A reporter for many years and the author of more than twenty books, Mr. Liston is currently living in Connecticut. His other books published by Franklin Watts, Inc. are *The Limits of Defiance: Rights, Strikes, and Government, The Edge of Madness: Prisons and Prison Reform in America,* and *The Right to Know: Censorship in America.*

ABOUT THE AUTHOR